W9-BAF-741

THE PRAYER OF JESUS

Secrets to Real Intimacy with God

Hank Hanegraaff

W PUBLISHING GROUP
A Division of Thomas Nelson Publishers
Since 1798

www.wpublishinggroup.com

DEDICATION

To my daughter Christina, who loves to pray.
Christ is not only foremost in her name but in her life.

THE PRAYER OF JESUS

Copyright © 2001 by Hank Hanegraaff. All rights reserved.
No portion of this publication may be reproduced, stored in
a retrieval system or transmitted in any form or by any
means—electronic, mechanical, photocopying, recording, or
any other—except for brief quotations in printed reviews,
without the prior written permission of the publisher.

Published by W Publishing Group, a Division of Thomas Nelson, Inc.,
P. O. Box 141000, Nashville, TN 37214.

W Publishing Group books may be purchased in bulk for educational,
business, fundraising, or sales promotional use. For information, please
e-mail SpecialMarkets@ThomasNelson.com.

All Scripture quotations in this book, except those
noted otherwise, are from the New International Version
of the Bible (NIV), copyright © 1983 by the International Bible Society.
Used by permission of Zondervan Bible Publishers.

ISBN 0-8499-0871-X (repack)
ISBN 0-8499-1730-1 (hc)

Printed and bound in the United States of America

02 03 04 05 06 BTY 12 11 10 9 8 7

Contents

FOREWORD

On November 8, 1981, after nearly two years of investigating the evidence for Christianity, I felt compelled to abandon my atheism and embrace Jesus as my Forgiver, Leader, and Friend. But then I was stuck. Now what?

How was I supposed to develop a relationship with an invisible God?

How could I converse with Jesus if I couldn't audibly hear his voice in return?

Why should I ask for something if God already knows my needs in advance?

Was I being selfish if I requested the desires of my heart? Was there a right way and a wrong way of talking to God?

There's no shortage of advice on prayer. Amazon.com

lists 8,202 books on the subject. How does anyone know what's valid and what isn't? Are there really short-cuts as some authors claim?

Frankly, I ended up treating prayer as if I were at a spiritual smorgasbord—I took a little of this author's ideas, a bit of advice from that pastor's sermons, applied some miscellaneous Bible verses, and mixed it with some counsel of well-meaning friends. The result: an imbalanced and half-baked prayer life that left me starving for something more satisfying.

It took me longer than I'd like to admit to seek counsel from the very One who is the ultimate expert on relating to God: Jesus Christ himself. I soon found that he had personally revealed the essentials of prayer. Thanks to his teaching and modeling, I now had a fully orbed way of deepening my relationship with God. The result has been the adventure of a lifetime!

And that's the approach my friend Hank Hanegraaff takes in his wonderfully insightful book *The Prayer of Jesus.* He lets the Master lay out a spiritual feast for anyone who wants to be truly nourished. In fact, I wish he had written it twenty years ago!

Hank has produced a balanced, practical, and very wise orientation to prayer. It flows not just from his considerable theological knowledge, but also from his personal experience in applying Jesus' principles day by day in his own life. I have prayed with him in quiet moments out of the spotlight. It's clear that prayer is not merely something he does, but a lifestyle he lives.

I'm thankful he did the hard work of keeping the book concise, focused, and accessible. He makes prayer simple, as it should be, but never simplistic. Ultimately, the depth of the book will be measured by the degree to which you put its Christ-centered teachings into practice in your everyday living. Believe me, the results will be exhilarating!

Polls tell us nearly everyone prays; personal experience tells us few are satisfied. *The Prayer of Jesus* will get you started in the right direction as you build a healthy and well-balanced prayer life that will honor God and serve you well for a lifetime.

So go ahead, turn the page. Let the adventure begin!

—LEE STROBEL

Acknowledgments

I'd first like to acknowledge Lee Strobel for his foreword and encouragement; the board and staff of the Christian Research Institute—especially Paul Young for his prayers, Stephen Ross for his insights, Elliott Miller for his edits, and Melanie Cogdill for her suggestions. Furthermore, I'd like to thank Bob and Gretchen Passantino for always being ready to brainstorm; Rick Dunham for his godly wisdom; Mark Sweeney, David Moberg, and the Word staff for their insights and support; and Mary Hollingsworth for her editing expertise. Finally, I would like to express my love and gratitude to Kathy and the kids—Michelle, Katie, David, John Mark, Hank Jr., Christina, Paul Stephen, Faith, and baby Grace, who preceded us to heaven. Above all, I am supremely thankful to the One who taught us the prayer of Jesus.

Introduction

Talk about dreaming the impossible dream! A book on prayer finally climbed its way past *Harry Potter and the Sorcerer's Stone* to sit atop the *New York Times* bestseller list.[1] And not just any book. It's a book chronicling the prayer of a little-known Old Testament character named Jabez, sandwiched in among hundreds of names in a long genealogical list. Yet amazingly, Jabez has achieved superstar status and spawned a virtual cottage industry of spin-off products.

Religion editor for *Publishers' Weekly*, Lynn Garrett, describes the book, simply titled *The Prayer of Jabez*,[2] as a "raging success," which will probably continue to build because "it's very evangelical and very American, this whole notion that if you know the right technique, the right form, that prayer will be efficient and effective. Kind of like golf."[3] *Time* notes that author Bruce Wilkinson ". . . sweetens his thesis with anecdotes from his personal and preaching life" and concludes "by claiming that daily recitation of the prayer can turn you into . . . someone like him."[4] Indeed, Wilkinson says he is proof of what can happen if you incorporate the Jabez prayer into your daily routine. And Wilkinson is not alone. Many people testify that they, like he, have achieved extraordinary success in life. One enthusiastic reader told me that she followed the simple formula prescribed in the book and that, as a result, her life was absolutely revolutionized. Each day for thirty days she disciplined herself to set aside the time to faithfully pray the prayer of Jabez. She taped the prayer to her bathroom mirror and kept a record of the divine appointments and new opportunities she experienced as a result.

Not everyone who encounters *The Prayer of Jabez,* however, is equally enthused. Like *PW's* Garrett, we have heard from some who say they see it as the quintessential example of fast-food Christianity. Others worry that *The Prayer of Jabez* relies more heavily on personal stories than on passages of Scripture.

Are such critiques fair? Has *Time* correctly characterized Jabez? Is this just another how-to formula—you know, "Pray this prayer once a day for thirty days and tell one other person about your 'new prayer habit,'" or could this really be "a God thing"? Given the hundreds of narratives containing incredibly significant prayers of biblical saints, why is it that so many millions are enamored with *this* prayer? More to the point, what would Jesus say about the prayer of Jabez? If we could ask him, "Lord teach us how to pray," would he tell us to pray the prayer of Jabez?

All these questions and a host of others flowed through my mind as calls and letters began flooding into the offices of the Christian Research Institute. While I was previously familiar with Jabez from a genealogical perspective, it had never occurred to me to ponder the spiritual implications of this one-sentence prayer squished in amongst hundreds of virtually unpronounceable names. However, the avalanche of correspondence, calls, and comments that cascaded down upon me renewed my respect for just how hungry people are to connect with God through prayer. So many expressed guilt for not making prayer a regular part of their daily routines. Bruce Wilkinson's astounding accomplishments have made us all aware of our own inadequacies. Like him, we desperately want our lives to count but often just can't seem to overcome inertia.

After reading *The Prayer of Jabez,* I was personally motivated to reexamine my own prayer life in light of Scripture. And it was from that study that this book was born.

As we once again renew our commitment to making prayer a priority, we want to know we are embarking on a journey that truly represents a major paradigm shift. As we progress we will take a closer look at prayer from the perspective of the Master Teacher, Jesus Christ. Of one thing we can be certain, when we ask him for bread, he will not give us a stone.

Join me as we embark upon a truly exhilarating expedition! An expedition that will demonstrate in spades that the thrill is not the destination but the journey—a journey that will impact your life not just for time but also for eternity. You are about to plug into the power, provision, and purpose of prayer, as only the Son of God can provide it. In the end you will understand how the prayer of Jesus is the pattern for not only your own prayer life but for truly understanding all of the other prayers recorded in Scripture.

CHAPTER ONE

Lord Teach Us Now to Pray

*He taught as one who had authority, and not as their
teachers of the law.*

—MATTHEW 7:29

You can almost see the sense of urgency sketched on the
faces of the disciples as they circle around the Master
Teacher. One of them, perhaps Peter, assumes the role of
spokesman. Instead of asking, "Lord, teach us *how* to
pray," he impetuously blurts out, "Lord, teach us *now* to
pray" (Luke 11:1)![1]

His words were both eager and expectant. Over and
over again he has watched the Master withdraw to
secluded places to pray. And he had seen the serenity
Jesus exuded in the aftermath. He may have been uncer-
tain of what made Christ's face seem as though it
glowed, but of one thing he was certain: Whatever it
was, he wanted it, and he wanted it *now!*

Jesus knew that his disciples would never properly understand **examples** *of prayer without first understanding* **principles** *of prayer.*

The disciples had, no doubt, previously heard Jesus preach about prayer when he presented his spellbinding Sermon on the Mount (Matthew 5–7). But that was a public sermon with the masses. This was an opportunity for a private session with the Master. And Jesus, sensing their urgency, knew he had their un-divided attention.

There were hundreds of scrip-tural prayers Jesus could have drawn their attention to that day. He might have highlighted the astonishing prayer of Solomon in the Second Book of Chronicles. Remember the story? God told Solomon to ask for whatever he wanted (2 Chronicles 1:7). Imagine that! Just name it and it's yours!

I don't know about you, but I can imagine myself blurting out, "Lord, bless me, and give me a better golf swing than even Tiger Woods so that I might win the Masters for your glory."

But not Solomon. He humbly asked for wisdom and

understanding instead (v.10). The Bible records that God was so pleased with his prayer that he not only made Solomon the wisest man who ever lived, but he blessed him with "riches, wealth and honor" (v.12). Talk about a formula for success!

Or Jesus might have responded by pointing his disciples to the prayers of Joshua, Jephthah, or, yes, Jabez. But he didn't. Jesus knew that his disciples would never properly understand *examples* of prayer without first understanding *principles* of prayer. And that's exactly why he gave us the prayer of Jesus.

He did not give us a prayer mantra; he gave us a prayer pattern. And the disciples learned it well. In fact, even a cursory reading of the epistles shows just how well. Within a few short years, they had turned the Roman Empire upside down! Just as the prayer of Jesus revolutionized their lives, it can transform yours.

Let me ask you a question: Was Peter speaking for you when he pleaded, "Lord, teach us *now* to pray?" Does Jesus have your undivided attention? Then turn the page and discover the very first secret of praying Jesus' way.

CHAPTER TWO

The Secret

But when you pray, go into your room, close the door and pray to your Father, who is unseen. Then your Father, who sees what is done in secret, will reward you.
—MATTHEW 6:6

Everyone wants to know the secret—you know, the secret to a successful marriage; the secret to raising happy kids; the secret to making a fortune on Wall Street; the secret to a perfectly sculptured body. The list is endless. I have to confess that I, too, have been looking for the secret—the secret to playing golf like Tiger Woods! Although golf has brought me great satisfaction over the years, it has been extremely frustrating as well. At times I feel as if I'm on the verge of setting a new course record. At other times, I wonder why I ever took up this sport in the first place.

Given my love for golf, you can imagine that when I heard that Tiger Woods and his coach, Butch Harmon, were going to talk about the secret to his success on *Golf Talk Live*, they had my undivided attention. I considered this the opportunity of a lifetime—a chance to learn the secret of golf from the greatest athlete on the planet. I have to confess I did my fair share of speculating. Perhaps Tiger's secret was the new Nike golf ball he was playing. Maybe it was the fact that Tiger's endorsement contracts allowed him to play without any pressure. Or maybe his coach had run across a little-known trade secret and had kept it from everyone else except Tiger.

I can still remember the anticipation I felt as I turned on the television and waited to hear "the secret." Within moments, however, my hopes were dashed as Tiger and his coach made it crystal clear that there were no shortcuts to golf. As the broadcast unfolded I learned that even someone as talented as Tiger had to spend months beating thousands of golf balls to make even the most nuanced change in his golf swing. More significantly, I learned that Tiger Woods loved his practice time in seclusion even more than the limelight of the cameras or the roaring approval of the crowds.

As I was writing, Tiger was on the brink of accom-

plishing the rarest feat in profes-
sional golf. In just moments he
would make history as the only
player in the modern era to hold
all four majors at once. U.S. Open-
champion-turned-broadcaster,

The secret to prayer is secret prayer.

Ken Venturi, looked dazed as he mumbled into his
microphone, "Something I never dreamt that I would
ever see, or anyone could ever do. I think that's the greatest feat I've ever known in all of sports." As Tiger sank
his final putt, Venturi exclaimed, "We just witnessed a
miracle!"

When Tiger was interviewed, however, a much-
needed perspective emerged. It was not a miracle. He
had performed in public the way he practiced in private.
At that very moment he was talking about a shot struck
on the thirteenth hole that was crucial to his victory. "It's
a shot I've been practicing the last couple of months,
knowing that I'm probably going to need that shot."[1] I
was amazed as I listened. Imagine practicing one shot
over and over again not just for days or for weeks but for
months. Suddenly I realized that Tiger was reiterating

the same principle he had shared earlier on *Golf Talk Live*. And in the process he was once again revealing the secret to success.

THE SECRET TO PRAYER IS SECRET PRAYER

Tiger's success in the Master's was directly attributable to the thousands of hours he spent practicing the game he loves in the secret place. Thus, his public performance was defined by his private practice. Likewise, the private prayer of Christians should define their public lives, not vice versa. The goal of prayer should never be the roaring approval of the crowds but rather the approval of our Father in heaven. As Jesus so eloquently put it, "When you pray, do not be like the hypocrites, for they love to pray standing in the synagogues and on the street corners to be seen by men. I tell you the truth, they have received their reward in full. But when you pray, go into your room, close the door and pray to your Father, who is unseen. Then your Father, who sees what is done in secret, will reward you." The secret to prayer is secret prayer.

Jesus provided the ultimate example. As Dr. Luke puts it, he "often withdrew to lonely places and prayed" (Luke 5:16). Unlike the religious leaders of his day, he did not pray to be seen by men. He prayed because he treasured fellowship with his Father. Hypocrites gain their reward through public prayer. They may be perceived as spiritual giants, but by the time they are finished, they have received everything they will ever get—their prayer's worth and nothing more.

Steeped in religious practices, these hypocrites tithed, fasted, and traveled "over land and sea" to win converts. They even prayed. And how! They prayed publicly in synagogues, and they prayed publicly on street corners. They even wore boxes on their foreheads containing pet prayers. Yet their motivation was not intimacy with God but to be seen by men. Thus, said Jesus, "They have received their reward in full."

PRAYER IS ITS OWN REWARD

For Tiger, playing golf is its own reward. It is obvious that he loves the *process* more than he loves the *prize*. For

*Prayer does not simply **maintain** the Christian life, it is the Christian life ...*

Christians, prayer should be its own reward. Prayer is not a magic formula to get things from God. Communing with God in prayer is itself the prize. As Philip Graham Ryken explains, "The reward for secret prayer is the prayer itself, the blessing of resting in the presence of God. Prayer does not simply *maintain* the Christian life, it *is* the Christian life, reduced to its barest essence. Can there be any greater joy—in this world or the next—than to commune in the secret place with the living God?"[2] The tragedy of contemporary Christianity is that we measure the success of our prayer life by the size and scope of our accomplishments, rather than the strength of our relationships with God. All too often we are fixated on our outwardness, while God is focused on our inwardness.

Why is it that modern-day athletes suffer from so many addictions? Could it be that they are laden with the trinkets of outward success but are often inwardly empty? Why do so many Christian leaders succumb to vices or affairs? Could it be that their adulteries spring out of outward achievements devoid of an inward connection with God through prayer? Could it be that the spiritual apathy of their souls leaves them vulnerable to the secondary appetites of the flesh?

As Calvin Miller has well said, "The absence of inwardness is the lost freedom we trade for addictions. Pascal was right. There is a God-shaped vacuum in our lives that only God can fill. . . . When God fills our inner vacuum with his Holy Spirit, life works. When God does not fill the vacuum, a host of consuming appetites swarm through our better intentions."[3] Miller adds, "It all adds up to a kind of powerlessness, which always results from living too far from the Grand Enabler. When we will not provide a place for the direction of the indwelling Christ, all that is left is the frenzied agenda of our hassled discipleship. The sad thing about all this is that true discipleship can never be frenzied, for it emulates its Master and turns from the turbulent to embrace a steady devotion and a silent adoration."[4]

The American sentiment that "bigger is better" has invaded our Christian subculture and seduced us to seek instant success through prayer mantras. Christian leaders all too often pray for masses and classes and in the end achieve little more than flashes and ashes. As human beings we want instant formulas, but God wants intimate fellowship. Says Miller, "We want to pray for a fiery chariot in the morning and be riding to church in it by nightfall. We rarely pray for fire and open our eyes to find a box of matches in our hand."[5]

> Thunderclaps and lightning flashes are very unlikely. It is well to start small and quietly. No need to tell one's friends and acquaintances. No need to plan heroic fasts or all-night vigils . . . prayer is neither to impress other people nor to impress God. It's not to be taken on with a mentality of success. The goal, in prayer, is to give oneself away.[6]

GOD ALWAYS RESPONDS

Not only is prayer its own reward, but secret prayer is always rewarded by a response from God. While the response we get is not always the response we want, it is the best response. A story Joni Eareckson Tada once told me aptly illustrates the point. Thirty years ago she became a quadriplegic as the result of a diving accident. Stuck in the geriatric ward of a state institution in Maryland, she would listen for hours as her friends read her stories from the Scriptures. One of her favorites was the story of a man who had been an invalid for thirty-eight years. Jesus encountered him lying by the Pool of Bethesda and healed him.

As a result of the story, Joni began picturing herself lying on a straw mat by the Pool of Bethesda. For hours on end she pleaded with God for a miraculous healing. It seemed in those days that God did not reward her prayer with a response. Thirty years later, however, she received a revelation of sorts during a trip to Jerusalem with her husband Ken. He pushed her wheelchair down the steps of the *Viá Dolorosa*, made a left turn at the sheep's gate, walked by St. Anne's church, and ran straight into the Pool of Bethesda. While resting her arms on the guard-rail overlooking those now dry, dusty ruins, Joni's mind flashed back to those thirty years earlier that she had pictured herself lying on a mat at this very place.

Rather than fixate on earthly vanities, such as the admiration of men, we ought to focus on such eternal verities as the approval of the Master.

Suddenly, like a thunderbolt across a clear blue sky, she was struck by the realization that God had not given her the response she was looking for. He had given her a far better one. Overwhelmed with emotion, she began to thank him for *not* healing her. God had miraculously turned her wheelchair into her secret place. That day Joni could have cried out, "O Wheelchair, I bless thee!" For it was in the prison of her wheelchair that she learned the secret of secret prayer.

Unable to run here and there with perfectly formed limbs, she spent hours practicing the principles of prayer. And as her life grew ever richer and deeper, she was enabled to bless multitudes out of the overflow of a life spent in the secret place. It was in her secret place that she discovered there were more important things than walking. And as she grew in intimacy with her Creator, she learned to bless the cross that crafted her character.

ETERNAL REWARDS

Finally, prayer leads to rewards in eternity. Christ's message is crystal clear. Rather than fixate on earthly vanities, such as the admiration of men, we ought to focus on such eternal verities as the approval of the Master. He warned his followers not to store up for themselves "treasures on earth, where moth and rust destroy, and where thieves break in and steal" (Matthew 6:19). Instead, said Jesus, store up "treasures in heaven, where moth and rust do not destroy, where thieves do not break in and steal" (v. 20). The rewards for a life of faithful prayer in the secret place involve not only enlarged responsibilities but enhanced spiritual capacities. As the capacity for enjoying music is greatly enhanced when one masters a musical instrument, the work we do here and now will greatly enhance our capacity for enjoying eternity.

In our fast-food culture we are forever looking for instant gratification. A cacophony of voices promise us quick fixes and instant cures when in reality there are none. The secret to a successful marriage is found in the time spent developing a relationship with your spouse. The secret to raising kids is a function of the quality and quantity of the time spent interacting with them. The secret to a successful portfolio is directly related to understanding the fundamentals of the companies in which you invest. The secret to a perfectly sculptured body is proper eating and exercise. The secret to Tiger's mastery of golf is the thousands of hours he spends practicing the fundamentals. And the secret to prayer is secret prayer.

CHAPTER THREE

Your Father Knows

And when you pray, do not keep on babbling like pagans, for they think they will be heard because of their many words. Do not be like them, for your Father knows what you need before you ask him.

—MATTHEW 6:31

Over sixty years ago a famous fictional character named Jabez Stone hit the big time in the Academy Award-winning movie *The Devil and Daniel Webster.* Stone wasn't evil, but he appeared to be the unluckiest man in all of New Hampshire. Unlike men who have the Midas touch, everything he touched turned to gravel in his teeth. One day he couldn't take it anymore. He had just broken his plowshare, his horse was sick, his children came down with the measles, his wife was ailing and he had just injured his hand. Although Stone was religious, that day he vowed he would sell his soul to the Devil for a shortcut to success in life.

The Devil obliged, and at the expense of his soul

promised to prosper Stone for seven years. Outwardly, Stone's life was immediately flooded with good fortune and all the trappings of success. Inwardly, however, his spirit had begun to shrivel up and die. He was about to gain the whole world but lose his very soul. As I watched the movie and read the famous short story by Stephen Vincent Benét on which the movie was based, I could not help but think back to the haunting words of Jesus, "You fool! this very night your life will be demanded from you" (Luke 12:20).

Like Stone, all of us have been tempted to look for shortcuts to success. And nowhere is this truer than when it comes to our prayer lives. We desperately want good fortune. We want a formula that will open up the windows of heaven and rain down its blessings. If you want to get right down to it, our prayers often sound dangerously close to the pleas of pagans, who constantly worry, saying, "What shall we eat? What shall we drink? What shall we wear" (Matthew 6:31)?

Thus, before Jesus launches into the principles of prayer through the most beautiful, symmetrical, and majestic of all biblical prayers, he first warns his disciples against praying as pagans do. The last thing he wants his disciples to do is turn the prayer he is about to teach them into what the New King James version of the Bible describes as "vain repetitions" (Matthew 6:7). So, says Jesus, "When you pray, do not keep on babbling like pagans, for they think they will be heard because of their many words. Do not be like them, for your Father knows what you need before you ask him" (vv. 7–8).

As the father of eight, I can tell you that I sometimes know what my children need before they ask me. However, what I, as an earthly father, only sometimes know, our eternal Father always knows. There's no need to pull out the prayer beads or attempt to wear God down by repeating the same prayers over and over. He already knows what you need before you ask him.

This statement by Christ inevitably leads to this question: Why bother praying if God knows what we need before we even ask him? I fear the very reason that this question is so often posed is that we have been conditioned to think that supplication is the sole sum and substance of prayer. The prayer of Jabez, now on the lips of multitudes, is an example of supplication.

If we are to nurture a strong bond with our Creator, we must continually communicate with him.

It is great to ask God to "bless me indeed" so that I can be a blessing to others. It is glorious that God should "enlarge my border" so that I might reach more people for his kingdom. It is right to ask that God's "hand might be with me" so that I might be led through the challenges of life by his sovereign control and not by chance. And it is proper to pray, "Keep me from harm that it may not pain me." Prayer, however, is not merely a means of presenting our requests, it is a means of pursuing a relationship with our heavenly Father.

As I write, the lyrics of a Country Western song, sung by Grammy Award-winning singer and song writer Paul Overstreet, wash through my mind.

"How much do I owe you," said the man to his Lord,
"For giving me this day, and all the days that's gone before?
Shall I build a temple, shall I make a sacrifice?
Tell me Lord, and I will pay the price.

And the Lord said,

"I won't take less than your love, sweet love.

No, I won't take less than your love.

All the treasures of this world could never be enough,

And I won't take less than your love.[1]

The point of the lyrics, which deal not only with the relationship of a man to his Lord but with the relationship of a husband to his wife and a mother to her son, is that relationships are cemented not just by giving and getting but by love and communication.

The fact that I often know what my kids are going to ask before they open their mouths does not mean I don't want them to ask. Rather, I long for them to verbalize their thoughts and feelings. That's how our relationship blossoms and grows. Likewise, if we are to nurture a strong bond with our Creator, we must continually communicate with him. And prayer is our primary way of doing just that. A memorable way of prioritizing the principles of such communication through prayer is found in the acronym F-A-C-T-S.[2]

FAITH

Faith is only as good as the object in which it is placed. Put another way, it is the object of faith that renders faith faithful. The secret is not in the phrases we utter but in coming to know ever more fully the One to whom we pray. Since God is awesomely revealed in his Word, the prayer of faith must always be rooted in Scripture. Prayer becomes truly meaningful when we enter into a relationship with God through Christ. We can then build on that foundation by saturating ourselves with Scripture. As R. A. Torrey so wonderfully expressed it:

> To pray the prayer of faith we must, first of all, study the Word of God, especially the promises of God, and find out what the will of God is. . . . We cannot believe by just trying to make ourselves believe. Such belief as that is not faith but credulity; it is "make believe." The great warrant for intelligent faith is God's Word. As Paul puts it in Romans 10:17, "Faith comes by hearing the message, and the message is heard through the word of Christ."[3]

Jesus summed up the prayer of faith with these words: "If you remain in me and my words remain in you, ask whatever you wish, and it will be given you" (John 15:7).

ADORATION

Faith in God naturally leads to adoration. Prayer without adoration is like a body without a soul. It is not only incomplete, but it just doesn't work. Through adoration we express our genuine, heartfelt love and longing for God. Adoration inevitably leads to praise and worship, as our thoughts are focused on God's surpassing greatness. The Scriptures are a vast treasury overflowing with descriptions of God's grandeur and glory. The Psalms, in particular, can be transformed into passionate prayers of adoration.

> Come, let us worship and bow down;
> Let us kneel before the Lord our Maker.
> For He is our God,
>   and we are the people of His pasture,
> And the sheep of His hand.
>
> —PSALM 95: 6–7 NASB

CONFESSION

Not only do the Psalms abound with illustrations of adoration, but they are replete with exclamations of confession as well. Those who are redeemed by the person and work of Jesus are positionally declared righteous before God. In practical terms, however, we are still sinners who sin every day. While unconfessed sin will not break our *union* with God, it will break our *communion* with God. Thus confession is a crucial aspect of daily prayer.

The concept of confession carries the acknowledgment that we stand guilty before God's bar of justice. There's no place for self-righteousness before God. We can only develop intimacy with the Lord through prayer when we confess our need for forgiveness and contritely seek his pardon. The Apostle John sums it up beautifully when he writes, "If we confess our sins, he is faithful and just and will forgive us our sins and purify us from all unrighteousness" (1 John 1:9).

THANKSGIVING

Nothing, and I mean nothing, is more basic to prayer

than thanksgiving. Scripture teaches us to "enter his gates with thanksgiving and his courts with praise" (Psalm 100:4). Failure to do so is the stuff of pagan babblings and carnal Christianity. Pagans, says Paul, know about God, but "they neither glorified him as God *nor gave thanks to him*" (Romans 1:21, emphasis added).

Carnal Christians likewise fail to thank God regularly for his many blessings. They suffer from what might best be described as selective memories and live by their feelings rather than by faith. They are prone to forget the blessings of yesterday as they thanklessly barrage the throne of grace with new requests each day.

That, according to the Apostle Paul, is a far cry from how we should pray. Instead we ought to approach God "overflowing with thankfulness"(Colossians 2:7) as we devote ourselves "to prayer, being watchful and thankful" (4:2). Such thankfulness is an action that flows from the sure knowledge that our heavenly Father knows exactly what we need and will supply it. Thus says Paul we are to " be joyful always; pray continually; give thanks in all circumstances, for this is God's will for you in Christ Jesus" (1 Thessalonians 5:16–18; also Ephesians 5:20).

SUPPLICATION

Before we launch into a discussion of the place and priority of supplication, let's quickly review the aspects of prayer we have covered thus far. We began by noting that prayer begins with a humble faith in the love and resources of our heavenly Father. Thus prayer becomes a means through which we learn to lean more heavily upon him and less heavily upon ourselves. Such faith inevitably leads to adoration as we express our longing for an ever deeper and richer relationship with the One who knit us together in our mothers' wombs. The more we get to know him in the fullness of his majesty, the more we are inclined to confess our unworthiness and to thank him not only for his saving and sanctifying grace but also for his goodness in supplying all our needs.

It is in the context of such a relationship that God desires that his children bring their requests before his throne of grace with praise and thanksgiving. After all it was Jesus himself who taught us to pray, "Give us this day our daily bread." And as we do we must ever be mindful of the fact that the purpose of supplication is not to pressure

God into providing us with provisions and pleasures, but rather to conform us to his purposes. As we read in 1 John 5:14–15, "This is the confidence we have in approaching God: that if we ask anything *according to his will,* he hears us. And if we know that he hears us—whatever we ask— we know that we have what we have asked of him" (emphasis added).

SO, WHY ASK?

This brings us back to the question posed earlier: If God knows what we need before we even ask, why bother asking at all? My initial response was a reminder that supplication is not the sole sum and substance of our prayers. Far from merely being a means of presenting our daily requests to God, it is a means of pursuing a dynamic relationship with him.

Furthermore, we should note that God ordains not only the ends but also the means. Thus, to ask, "Why pray if God knows what we need?" is akin to asking, "Why get dressed in the morning and go to work?" For that matter, if God is going to do what he's going to do anyway, why

We must ever be mindful of the fact that the purpose of supplication is not to pressure God into providing us with provisions and pleasures, but rather to conform us to his purposes.

bother doing anything? As C.S. Lewis once put it, "Why, then, do we not argue as the opponents of prayer argue, and say that if the intended result is good God will bring it to pass without your interference, and that if it is bad He will prevent it happening whatever you do? Why wash your hands? If God intends them to be clean, they'll come clean without your washing them. If He doesn't, they'll remain dirty (as Lady Macbeth found)[4] however much soap you use. Why ask for the salt? Why put on your boots? Why do anything?"[5] Lewis provides the answer as follows:

> We know that we can act and that our actions produce results. Everyone who believes in God must therefore admit (quite apart from the question of prayer) that God has not chosen to write the whole of history with his own hand. Most of the events that go on in the uni-

verse are indeed out of our control, but not all. It is like a play in which the scene and the general outline of the story are fixed by the author, but certain minor details are left for the actors to improvise. It may be a mystery why He should have allowed us to cause real events at all; but it is no odder that He should allow us to cause them by praying than by any other method.

He gave us small creatures the dignity of being able to contribute to the course of events in two different ways. He made the matter of the universe such that we can (in those limits) do things to it; that is why we can wash our own hands and feed or murder our fellow creatures. Similarly, He made His own plan or plot of history such that it admits a certain amount of free play and can be modified in response to our prayers.[6]

Lewis goes on to explain that God has ordained that the work we do and the prayers we utter both produce results. If you pull out a weed, it will no longer be there. If you drink excessively, you will ruin your health. And if you waste planetary resources, you will shorten the life-line of history. There is, however, a substantive difference between what happens as a result of our work and what happens as a result of our prayers. The result of pulling up a weed is "divinely guaranteed and therefore ruthless." Thankfully, however, the result of prayer is not. God has left himself discretionary power to grant or refuse our requests, without which prayer would destroy us. Says Lewis,

It is not unreasonable for a headmaster to say, "Such and such things you may do according to the fixed rules of this school. But such and such other things are too dangerous to be left to general rules. If you want to do them you must come and make a request and talk over the whole matter with me in my study. And then —we'll see."7

Let me make one final point before we move to the pattern and principles of the prayer Jesus taught his disciples. While our Father knows what we need before we even ask, our supplications are in and of themselves an acknowledgement of our dependence on him. And that alone is reason enough to pray without ceasing.

Chapter Four

Building Our Relationship

Our Father in heaven, hallowed be your name.
—Matthew 6:9

A father was overheard giving his son a tongue lashing for being so biblically illiterate. "You probably don't even know the Lord's Prayer," he shouts sarcastically. "Oh yes I do," the boy retorts triumphantly. "Now I lay me down to sleep, I pray the Lord my soul to keep. If I should die before I wake, I pray the Lord my soul to take." Surprised, the father stammers, "Sorry son. I had no idea that you actually knew it."[1]

While this story is humorous, it is also heartrending. When I first heard it, I honestly did not know whether to laugh or cry. It is tragic to think that, in some circles, the Lord's prayer has been reduced to vain repetition, while in others it has been all but forgotten, despite the fact that it is the very prayer Jesus himself modeled. While he may have never prayed the prayer word for word himself, he did employ every glorious aspect of it in his personal prayer life. Thus, it can rightly be referred to as the prayer of Jesus.

THE PRAYER JESUS PRAYED

Philip Graham Ryken points out that it has become "fashionable to deny that the Lord's Prayer really is the *Lord's* prayer. Some prefer to call it the 'Disciples' Prayer' because, they say, Jesus himself never could have prayed the Lord's Prayer."[2] Ryken goes on to note that those who argue this way point out that Jesus could never have prayed, "Forgive us our debts as we have forgiven our debtors," because, as the perfect Man, he had no debts for which to be forgiven.

Let's stop and take a second look. Christ invaded time and space to assume our debts. Thus, "when Jesus died on the cross, was he not asking his Father—at least with his actions, if not with his words—to forgive us our debts? He was not seeking forgiveness for his own sins, but for our sins, which he had taken upon himself.

Furthermore, even while he was asking God to forgive our debts, Jesus forgave his debtors."[3]

Jesus modeled the other principles of the prayer he taught his disciples as well. When he taught his disciples to pray, "Our Father in heaven, hallowed be your name," it was because he himself prayed that way. In Christ's longest recorded prayer, he addressed God as "Father" at least a half a dozen times (John 17). At one point he even used the phrase "Holy Father," which is tantamount to saying, "Hallowed be thy name."

In the Garden of Gethsemane he not only addressed God as Father, but as he had taught his disciples to pray, "your kingdom come, your will be done," he now prayed, "if it is possible, may this cup be taken from me. *Yet not as I will, but as you will*" (Matthew 26:39, emphasis added).

Further, Jesus, though he was the Bread of Life, thanked God before he ate. He thanked God before he fed the five thousand (John 6:11) and when he broke bread with his disciples during the Last Supper (Matthew 26:26). Even after his resurrection he "took bread, gave thanks, broke it and began to give it" to his disciples (Luke 24:30).

While the prayer of Jesus is not a prayer **mantra,** *it is a prayer* **manner.**

Finally, Jesus taught his disciples to pray, "And lead us not into temptation but deliver us from the evil one," for he himself knew what it was to be tempted. Matthew writes, "Then Jesus was led by the Spirit into the desert to be tempted by the devil. After fasting forty days and forty nights, he was hungry. The tempter came to him and said, "'If you are the Son of God, tell these stones to become bread'" (Matthew 4:1–3). Likewise, Jesus, knowing that the Devil would tempt Simon Peter to deny him, prayed that Peter would be delivered from the evil one and that his faith would not fail (Luke 22:31–32).[4]

Jesus made every word he spoke count. The words of the prayer he taught us to pray are treasures of incalculable value lying deep beneath the cobalt waters of a vast ocean. Like the siren call of the mermaids, his words beckon those snorkeling with burnt backs in shallow tide pools to don scuba gear and descend into the prayer's glorious depths. There await unfathomed resources and riches that can scarcely be described to those living on the surface. While the prayer of Jesus is not a prayer *mantra,* it is a prayer *manner.* As such, it has been eloquently described as the most majestic of all model prayers:

It is a model prayer and, as such, commends itself to the most superficial glance—approves itself at once to the conscience of man. It is beautiful and symmetrical, like the most finished work of art. The words are plain and unadorned, yet majestic; and so transparent and appropriate that, once fixed in the memory, no other expressions ever mix themselves up with them; the thought of substituting other words never enters the mind. Grave and solemn are the petitions, yet the serenity and tranquil confidence, the peace and joy which they breathe, prove attractive to every heart.

The Prayer is short, that it may be quickly learned, easily remembered, and frequently used; but it contains all things pertaining to life and godliness. In its simplicity it seems adapted purposely for the weakness of the inexperienced and ignorant, and yet none can say that he is familiar with the heights and depths which it reveals, and with the treasures of wisdom it contains. It is calm, and suited to the even tenor of our daily life, and yet in times of trouble and conflict the church has felt its value and power more especially, has discovered anew that it anticipates every difficulty and danger, that it solves every problem, and comforts the disciples of Christ in every tribulation of the world.

It is the beloved and revered friend of our childhood, and it grows with our growth, a never-failing counselor and companion amid all the changing scenes of life. And as in our lifetime we must confess ourselves, with Luther, to be only learning the high and deep lessons of those petitions, so it will take eternity to give them their answer.[5]

OUR FATHER IN HEAVEN

To the disciples, the first words of the prayer of Jesus must have been nothing short of scandalous. Of all the things they had ever learned about prayer, this was certainly not one of them. They were not even permitted to say the name of God aloud, let alone refer to him as "our Father." Yet, that is precisely how Jesus taught his disciples to pray.

There was, however, a catch. As John explains, only those who received Jesus and believed on his name had the right to refer to God as "our Father" (see John 1:12). In fact, Jesus made it clear that there were only two kinds of people in the world: those who should refer to Satan as "our father" and those who may refer to God as "our Father" (John 8:44–47). There are no other options.

In one sense, Jesus is the only one who could legitimately address God as Father, for he is the unique Son of God and has been so throughout eternity. However, as Paul explains in Romans 8, those who are led by the Spirit of God are no longer illegitimate children. Instead, they, too, are sons and daughters by adoption through faith in Jesus. Thus, they can legitimately refer to God as "our Father."

Jesus continues the pattern by teaching his disciples to qualify the phrase "our Father" with the words "in heaven." In doing so he is teaching us that God transcends time and space. We can address him with intimacy but never with impudence. He is the sovereign Creator, and we are but sinful creatures. Addressing God as "our Father" makes us ever mindful of our relationship with God. It also underscores the fact that I do not come before him in isolation, rather I come as part of a community of faith. Thus, adding the phrase "in heaven" reminds us of the reverence due his name.

HALLOWED BE YOUR NAME

The initial request of the prayer of Jesus is that God's name be made holy. To pray "hallowed be your name" is to put the emphasis on God first, exactly where it belongs. Our daily lives should radiate a far greater commitment to God's nature and holiness than to our own needs. To pray "hallowed be your name" is to pray that God be given the unique reverence that his holiness demands; that God's Word be preached without corruption; that our churches be led by faithful pastors and preserved from false prophets; that we be kept from language that profanes God's name; that our thought lives remain holy; and that we cease from seeking honor for ourselves and seek instead that God's name be glorified.

In the words of Augustine, "This is prayed for, not as if the name of God were not holy already, but that it may be held holy by men; [in other words], that God may so become known to them, that they shall reckon nothing more holy, and which they are more afraid of offending."[6] Our monikers and meager attempts at ministry are meaningless unless God's name is magnified. As R. C. Sproul said, "Where God is not respected, it is inevitable that his image-bearers will also suffer a loss of respect."[7]

Our monikers and meager attempts at ministry are meaningless unless God's name is magnified.

The glorious truth of this petition is that while we were once impotent to hallow his name, God has hallowed us through the sacrifice of the very One who taught us these words. Once his light shining into our darkness would have been terrifying. But like Isaiah he has touched our lips with a burning coal and whispers through our pain, "Your guilt is taken away and your sin atoned for" (Isaiah 6:7). Puritan writer Thomas Watson assures us that, while some petitions are locked in time, this one is timeless:

When some of the other petitions shall be useless and out of date, as we shall not need to pray in heaven, "Give us our daily bread," because there shall be no sin; nor, "Lead us not into temptation," because the old serpent is not there to tempt: yet the hallowing of God's name will be of great use and request in heaven; we shall be ever singing hallelujahs, which is nothing else but the hallowing of God's name.[8]

CHAPTER FIVE

The City of God

Your kingdom come,
your will be done
on earth as it is in heaven.
—MATTHEW 6:10

YOUR KINGDOM COME

The phrase "your kingdom come" is gilded with such gold and glory that I scarcely know where to begin. I almost feel as if I am at Disney World with my kids and don't know which exhibit or ride will cause their eyes to sparkle more. Knowing that, in a few short paragraphs, I am unable to fully mine the vast storehouse of treasure locked up in this phrase, I can but console myself in praying that we will spend the rest of our lives wandering through its vastness enjoying its wisdom and its wealth.

To my kids the Magic Kingdom is heaven on earth. To me it's more like eternal conscious torment. I love to

At present, we are sandwiched between the triumph of the cross and the termination of time—between D-day and V-day.

see the smiles on their faces, but standing in line hour after hour in suffocating heat has left me wondering if that might well be what hell is like. One thing's for certain, as far as I'm concerned, the Magic Kingdom is definitely not heaven on earth.

Heaven once did exist on earth, however. But it didn't last long. The first human beings sinned and succeeded in dooming the planet. The rest of history has been a war between two kingdoms. In *The City of God* Augustine describes these kingdoms as the kingdom of God and the kingdom of man. "Each of these two kingdoms has its own ruler, its own people, its own desire, and its own destiny."[1]

In the fullness of time, God sent his Son into the world to overthrow the Devil's domain by driving out demons, performing miracles, preaching the good news of the coming kingdom, and ultimately sacrificing himself upon a cross. While Jesus came to establish an eternal kingdom, his subjects merely wanted an earthly king who would overthrow their enemies by military might.

Thus, when the Savior said, "My kingdom is not of this world" (John 18:36), the shouts of "Hosanna! Blessed is the King of Israel!" (John 12:13) changed to the screams of "Crucify him! We have no king but Caesar" (John 19:15)! They wanted an earthly king who would expand their earthly territory. Jesus, however, had come to take his rightful place on the throne of their lives.

In teaching us to pray "your kingdom come," Jesus was first and foremost teaching us to petition our heavenly Father to expand his rule over the territory of our hearts. It is an invitation to embrace the kingdom of Christ in every aspect of our lives. Like Stone in *The Devil and Daniel Webster*, we are called to renounce our deal with the Devil and pledge our allegiance to expand his kingdom rather than our own.

Furthermore, to pray "your kingdom come" is to pray that God would use our witness for the expansion of his kingdom. C.S. Lewis describes this world as "enemy occupied territory" and Christianity as "the story of how the rightful king has landed in disguise and is calling us all to take part in a great campaign of sabotage."[2]

Finally, to pray "your kingdom come" is to recognize that Christ has already won the war, but the reality of his reign is not yet fully realized. At present we are sandwiched between the triumph of the cross and the termination of time—between D-day and V-day. "D-day was the first coming of Christ, when the enemy was decisively defeated; V-day is the Second Coming of Christ, when the enemy shall totally and finally surrender."[3] This point is driven home by a comparison to the Nazi occupation of Norway:

Hitler had occupied Norway, but in 1945 it was liberated. Suppose that up in the almost inaccessible north some small village with a Nazi overlord failed to hear the news of the liberation for some weeks. During that time, we might put it, the inhabitants of the village were living in the "old" time of Nazi occupation instead of the "new" time of Norwegian liberation. . . . Any person who now lives in a world that has been liberated from the tyranny of evil powers either in ignorance of, or in indifference to, what Christ has done, is precisely in the position of those Norwegians to whom the good news of deliverance had failed to penetrate.[4]

History is hurtling towards a glorious and climactic end when the kingdoms of this world will become the kingdoms of our Lord. Jesus not only taught the Apostle John to pray "your kingdom come" but also gave him a glimpse of that kingdom on the Isle of Patmos. Says John, "I saw the Holy City, the new Jerusalem, coming down out of heaven from God, prepared as a bride beautifully dressed for her husband. And I heard a loud voice from the throne saying, 'Now the dwelling of God is with men, and he will live with them. They will be his people, and God himself will be with them and be their God. He will wipe every tear from their eyes. There will be no more death or mourning or crying or pain, for the old order of things has passed away" (Revelation 21:2–4). On that day, heaven will once again exist on earth.

YOUR WILL BE DONE

Everyone is familiar with the word "amen." But have you ever taken the time to consider what it really means? Amen is a universally recognized word that is far more significant than simply signing off or saying, "That's all." With the word "amen" we are in effect saying, "May it be so in accordance with the will of God." It is a marvelous reminder that any discussion on prayer must begin with the understanding that prayer is a means of bringing us into conformity with God's will, not a magic mantra that ensures God's conformity to ours.

Jesus is the very personification of the word "amen." In Revelation he is referred to as the "Amen, the faithful and true witness, the ruler of God's creation" (Revelation 3:14). And he not only taught us to pray "Your will be done," he modeled these words in his life. In his passionate prayer in the Garden of Gethsemane, he prayed, "My Father, if it is possible, may this cup be taken from me. Yet *not as I will, but as you will*"(Matthew 26:39, emphasis added). While Jesus may be our greatest example, he is certainly not our only example. His brother James warns those who are prone to "boast and brag" that they ought to pray instead, "If it is the Lord's will, we will live and do this or that" (James 4:15).

Christ's closest friend during his earthly ministry, the Apostle John, echoes the words of the Master when he writes, "This is the confidence we have in approaching God: that if we ask anything *according to his will,* he hears us" (1 John 5:14, emphasis added). Likewise, the Apostle Paul earnestly prayed that "by God's will" he might have the

We would be in deep trouble if God gave us everything for which we asked.

opportunity to visit the believers in Rome (Romans 1:10) and encouraged the believers in Rome to pray that "by God's will" he might come to visit them (Romans 15:32).

To pray "your will be done" is, first and foremost, recognition of the sovereignty of God. In effect it is a way of saying, "Thank God this world is under his control not mine!" We would be in deep trouble if God gave us everything for which we asked. The truth is we don't know what's best for us. As Dr. Gordon Fee has well said, "Our asking is based on our own limited knowledge, and all too often it is colored by our self-interest. We can only praise God that he does not answer every prayer 'prayed in faith.' Hezekiah, after all, had his prayer answered and was granted fifteen more years, but it was during those years that Manasseh was born!"5

The tragedy is not in dying young, but in living large and never using your life for eternal significance.

In retrospect, if Hezekiah had known, as God did, that in those fifteen additional years he would father the most wicked king in the history of Judah, position his kingdom for plunder by the Babylonians, and end up dying with his heart lifted up in pride, he may have well added these words to his prayer: "Nevertheless, not my will but thy will be done."

Furthermore, to pray "your will be done" is daily recognition that our wills must be submitted to his will. One of the most comforting thoughts that can penetrate a human mind yielded to the will of God is that he who has created us also knows what's best for us. Thus, if we walk according to his will, rather than trying to command him according to our own wills, we will indeed have, as he promised, not a panacea, but peace in the midst of storm.

In the yielded life there is great peace in knowing that the one who taught us to pray "your will be done" has every detail of our lives under control. Not only is he the object of our faith, he is also the originator of our faith. Indeed, he is the originator of our salvation and, yes, even the originator of our prayers. Thus, whatever we pray for, whether it's healing or a house, when our will is in harmony with his will, we will receive what we request one hundred percent of the time.

However, when we pray earnestly, as Christ did, "nevertheless not my will but thy will be done," we can rest assured that even in sickness and tragedy "all things work together for good to those who love God and are called according to his purpose" (Romans 8:28).

Finally, to pray "your will be done" is daily recognition that God will not spare us from trial and tribulation but rather use the fiery furnace to purge impurities from our lives. Charles Haddon Spurgeon, well known as the Prince of Preachers, was severely afflicted with gout, a condition that sometimes brings on excruciating pain.

In a sermon published in 1881 he wrote, "Were you ever in the melting pot, dear friends? I have been there, and my sermons with me. . . . The result of melting is that we arrive at a true valuation of things [and] we are poured out into a new and better fashion. And, oh, we may almost wish for the melting-pot if we may but get rid of the dross, if we may but be pure, if we may but be fashioned more completely like unto our Lord!"[6]

Spurgeon did not live a long, robust life. In fact, it may be said that he had everything except his health. At age 57 he died. Yet while he lived, he made his life count. He is history's most widely read preacher. His sermon series stand as the largest set of books by a single author in the history of the Christian church. Spurgeon's life bears eloquent testimony that the tragedy is not in dying young, but in living large and never using your life for eternal significance.

Ultimately, this is the message of the Book of Job. Job endured more tragedy in a single day than most people experience in a lifetime. Yet, in his darkest hour, Job would utter the ultimate words of faith: "Though he slay me yet will I trust in him" (Job 13:15). When we reach the end of this majestic literary masterpiece, we finally understand. Like a refreshing drink of water on a dry dusty day, our thirst for answers is quenched. He is sovereign. We are not. In this world you will have trouble (John 16:33). Disease, decay, disorder, discouragement and even death are the natural consequences of a fallen world. But as the Master so eloquently put it, "Take heart, I have overcome the world." For the child of God the hope is not perfect health and happiness in this lifetime but a resurrected body and a heavenly dwelling in the life to come.

ON EARTH AS IT IS IN HEAVEN

Allow me to make one quick point before we move on. As we pray we must be ever mindful that the phrase "in heaven" is inextricably woven together with each of the first three petitions of the prayer of Jesus. We begin by praying that the name of our Father *in heaven* be hallowed. We continue by praying, "Your kingdom come on earth as it is *in heaven*." And we conclude with the words "Your will be done on earth as it is *in heaven*."

This, of course, is not by accident. Rather it is a daily reminder that we are to live with heaven in mind. As we launch into the last three petitions of the prayer of Jesus, in which the Master teaches us how to bring our requests to God, we should never lose sight of our priorities. R.C. Sproul, in his inimitable style, makes the point, "We do not come rushing into God's presence arrogantly, assaulting Him with our petty requests, forgetting whom we are addressing. We are to make certain that we have properly exalted the God of creation. Only after God has been rightly honored, adored, and exalted, do the subsequent petitions of God's people assume their proper place."[7]

The prayer of Jesus is divided into essentially two parts. The first is focused on God's glory. Thus, we pray, "hallowed be *your* name, *your* kingdom come, *your* will be done." The second is focused on our needs. "From this point on we will pray for ourselves—our provision, our pardon, and our protection. It is the third petition that brings the Lord's Prayer down to earth, making the transition from our Father up in heaven to his children down on earth."[8] In the words of the great church father Tertullian:

> How gracefully has the Divine Wisdom arranged the order of the prayer; so that *after* things heavenly—that is, after the "Name" of God, the "Will" of God, and the "Kingdom" of God—it should give earthly necessities also room for a petition![9]

CHAPTER SIX

Bringing Our Requests

Give us today our daily bread.
—MATTHEW 6:11

Remember the scene from Luke 11 that I described in chapter one? Jesus has just returned from one of his private prayer sessions, his face awash with the glory of his Father's presence. The disciples immediately encircle him. One of them, perhaps Peter, verbalizes the words, but they were all thinking the same thing. "Lord," he says in a voice mixed with urgency and anticipation, "whatever it is you experience when you disappear for those long stretches and pray, we really want to know about it."

Jesus smiles. The time has come for him to unveil the principles of prayer to his disciples. As usual, he begins with a story. Pointing to Peter, he says, "Imagine going to your neighbor's house at midnight and asking him if you

Ask and it will be given to you; seek and you will find; knock and the door will be opened to you.

can borrow three loaves of bread." A smile breaks out on Thomas's face. He can't help but chuckle at the irony of the Bread of Life telling a story about borrowing bread.

"Your neighbor is fast asleep," Jesus continues, "so you pound on the door frantically and shout, 'Wake up! I need your help! A friend of mine has just shown up on my doorstep, and my cupboard is bare!'"

Jesus cups his hands around his mouth for effect. "'Don't bother me!' the neighbor yells back. 'I've locked up the house and my kids are in bed. I just can't help you tonight.'"

Peter wasn't very good at keeping a poker face. His thoughts might as well have been three-inch neon letters flashing across his forehead. "Yeah, right," Peter murmurs to himself, "this guy can't help? Or won't!" James and John locked eyes knowingly. *If Peter knocked on my door in the middle of the night,* they each were thinking, *I wouldn't get up either!*

"I tell you the truth," Jesus explains, "if Peter had just kept banging on the door, his neighbor would have given him bread. Not so much because he was a good neighbor, but because of Peter's persistence."

The disciples had begun to fidget. They didn't quite understand what Jesus meant.

"So I say to you: Ask and it will be given to you; seek and you will find; knock and the door will be opened to you. For anyone who asks receives; he who seeks finds; and to him who knocks, the door will be opened.

"If your grumpy neighbor offers you aid as a result of your persistence—if only to keep you from continuing to bother him—how much more will your heavenly Father, who is righteous and loving, come to your aid when you ask."

Some of the disciples were beginning to catch the meaning of the parable. Peter couldn't help himself. "I get it!" he shouted, his voice echoing through the canyon. "You're contrasting my grumpy neighbor with God." James, John, and the rest of the disciples now caught the full force of the meaning as well. Jesus was not *comparing* Peter's neighbor to God. He was *contrasting* the neighbor's grumpiness and resistance with God's goodness and readiness to help.

Jesus had just offered his disciples what is known as a lesser-to-greater argument for trusting God in prayer. If the lesser individual, the grumpy neighbor, was in the end willing to help a hungry man, *even for a less than noble reason,* how much more will our gracious heavenly Father respond when we humbly come before him and ask for our daily bread?

GIVE US TODAY OUR DAILY BREAD

Jesus does not want to leave his disciples wondering whether or not they have properly perceived the point of his parable. So he continues, "Which of you fathers, if your son asks for a fish, will give him a snake instead? Or if he asks for an egg, will give him a scorpion? If you then, though you are evil, know how to give good gifts to your children, how much more will your Father in heaven give the Holy Spirit to those who ask him?"

Jesus has just intensified the force of his story by moving from a relationship between neighbors to a relationship

between a father and his child. And
the message is beginning to resonate with his disciples. They have
been conditioned to think that
God was unapproachable; so if
they did ask him for anything, they
had better make it snappy.

*God promises to
provide the*
necessities, *but
not always the*
niceties.

Jesus, however, tells them that God cares for them as
a father cares for his own dear children. When we ask for
such essentials as our daily bread, our heavenly Father
will not turn his relationship with us into an illusion by
giving us something harmful, such as a scorpion or a
snake. Jesus puts an exclamation point on the parable by
drawing the attention of his disciples to the greatest gift
of all—the gift of the precious Holy Spirit.

As the Holy Spirit is an all-encompassing gift, so too
we are reminded that petitioning our heavenly Father to
"give us today our daily bread" encompasses far more than
food. As the great sixteenth century theologian Martin
Chemnitz once put it, "The word 'bread' in this petition
encompasses all things belonging to and necessary for the
sustenance of this body and life."[1]

Chemnitz goes on to underscore the fact that biblically the word "bread," in the context of the prayer of Jesus, can be rightly understood in a larger sense as "all those things that are required for the necessary, peaceable, and honest ordering of this life. This applies to the nation, the family, the productivity of the ground, profitable weather, and so on."[2] Note carefully the word "necessary." God promises to provide "the *necessities,* but not always the *niceties.*"[3] And we should want it no other way. With Agur, we should pray, "Give me neither poverty nor riches, but give me only my daily bread. Otherwise, I may have too much and disown you and say, 'Who is the Lord?' Or I may become poor and steal, and so dishonor the name of my God" (Proverbs 30:8–9).

Furthermore, when we ask our heavenly Father to "give us today our daily bread," we are praying in plural. Not only are we praying for the needs of our immediate family, but we are praying for the needs of our extended family as well. We do not pray as mere rugged individualists but as members of a community of faith. All we need do is turn on the television to see that our sisters and brothers around the world suffer daily from maladies ranging from droughts to deadly diseases. Yet, all too quickly, these images fade from our minds before the next commercial interruption.

Just a few moments ago I finished wolfing down a take-out meal from California Pizza Kitchen. All that was left were two slices of freshly baked bread. Since I've been writing for over a week with no exercise, I hardly dared eat another bite. So I walked out of my office and gave the bread to someone passing by. While hardly a sacrifice, it served as a subtle reminder that we cannot rightly pray *give* and not be *givers* ourselves.

In Luke 12 Jesus tells a there-are-no-moving-vans-following-hearses story. God had richly blessed a man, but his priorities were all out of whack. His rhetoric about his fortune was laced with self-interest—*my* grain, *my* goods, *my, my, my.* There was nothing wrong with how he had gained his wealth—no hint of impropriety or immorality. The problem was that he had purposed in his heart to "take life easy; eat, drink, and be merry" (v. 19), and in the process he had become insensitive to the needs of others. Jesus' condemnation was not only crisp and clear, it was downright chilling. "You fool!" he said. "This very night your life will be demanded of you" (v. 20).

Finally, when Jesus taught his disciples to pray "give us today our daily bread," he was reminding them that he was there to sustain them spiritually as well as physically. Each time we partake of communion we are reminded that he is "the bread of life" (John 6:35). As Ryken rightly reminds us, "When we receive communion, the bread on the table is physical bread, but it also has a spiritual meaning. The bread is an aftertaste of salvation. It reminds us of the Body that was given for our sins on the cross. It is also a foretaste of the kingdom to come, when we will sit down with Jesus at his eternal banquet and eat the bread of heaven."[4]

CHAPTER SEVEN

The Compassion Award

Forgive us our debts,
as we also have forgiven our debtors.
—MATTHEW 6:12

The deadline for finishing this book loomed ominously on the horizon. I have to confess that I was feeling more than just a little overwhelmed. I had asked my assistant to clear my schedule and hold my calls. I was deeply immersed in writing when suddenly I was jarred by the intrusive sound of the telephone.

"Where are you?" exclaimed a familiar voice.

Where am I? What do you mean "Where am I?" I thought to myself. Fortunately, I had learned long ago not to verbalize such unedited thoughts. My wife, Kathy, was on the other end of the line, and her tone of voice let me know I was in a world of trouble.

"I'm at the office, Honey," I replied cautiously.

"Well, you're supposed to be at school!" she replied with an edge to her voice. "Your daughter is about to receive a Compassion Award."

If there was one thing I had learned about Kathy over the years, it was that I could forget an anniversary or two, but missing a monumental moment in the life of one of our children might well qualify as an unforgivable sin.

"I'll be right over," I said, trying to mask my growing frustration. I rushed out of the office, hopped into the car, and sped toward school. As I was getting out of the car, though, my heart sank. Already I could see parents and their children swarming out of the auditorium. Not only had I succeeded in missing an important event in my daughter's life, but now I risked missing a book deadline as well.

I was not looking forward to seeing the you-should-have-been-here look on Kathy's face. Even more, I dreaded seeing the look of disappointment in my daughter's eyes. To my surprise, Kathy emerged from the crowd with a big smile.

"Lucky for you," she said playfully, "I caught the whole thing on tape."

"Sorry," I ventured sheepishly.

"That's all right, Sweetheart," she replied, "I know how busy you are right now."

Kathy's cheery disposition should have made me feel better, but it didn't. I was beginning to feel worse by the second. How could I have been too busy to attend something so important in my daughter's life?

Kathy's words interrupted my thoughts. "Don't beat yourself up," she said, sensing my remorse. "Go find Christina and give her a big hug. We can go back to your office and watch the tape together in a few minutes."

While thankful for Kathy's encouragement, my mind kept flashing back to the early morning hours. I remembered Christina looking into my eyes as I brushed her hair. Her words echoed in my head: "You're going to be there, right Daddy? You're going to come to my . . ." Suddenly I was struck by the realization that it wasn't her words that bothered me most—it was mine. "Sure, honey," I had replied confidently.

I didn't have to look far to find Christina. I had no

sooner turned around than she bounced into my arms and kissed me on the forehead. "Sorry I missed your award presentation," I said gently.

"That's all right, Daddy," she said, as she squeezed my neck. She didn't have to say another word. From the look in her eyes, it was obvious that she had already forgiven me.

I couldn't wait to see the video, as we hurried back to my office. I shoved the tape into the VCR and sat down next to Kathy on the couch. Within moments I was struggling to choke back tears.

Christina's teacher, Mrs. James, was saying, "There are two things I see in this young lady that I thought merited the Compassion Award. The first is that Christina is a constant source of encouragement to the adults and children at our school."

She gave some illustrations and then continued. "But there's a way that we can show compassion that nobody knows about but God, and that's what this young lady does. Christina does what Jesus tells us all to do in Mark 11:25, when he says, 'And when you stand praying, if you hold anything against anyone, forgive him, so that your Father in heaven may forgive you your sins.' And that's what she does—she forgives anybody who does wrong to her. She forgives them in her heart. She talks to the Lord about it, and then when she prays she knows her prayers are answered. . . ."

As I continued to watch the award presentation, I was struck by the realization that God had answered my prayers, too. That very morning before leaving for work I had pleaded for his wisdom as I began writing on the subject of forgiveness.

I shook my head as a smile crept over my face. I thought going to Christina's Compassion Award presentation would keep me from maintaining my writing schedule. Instead, God had used it to give me a real life example of forgiveness in action.

I turned toward Kathy and gave her a big hug. "Thanks for keeping my priorities in line," I murmured.

"Better get back to your writing," she said knowingly.

The words of the teacher were still ringing in my ears as I sat down to write. Her comments about Christina's willingness to forgive others were reminiscent of the closing statement of one of the most riveting parables Jesus ever communicated to his disciples.

It was the story of two debtors. The first owed his master about twenty million dollars—more than he could pay if he lived to be a thousand years old. The second debtor owed the first debtor less than a twenty-dollar bill. When the day of reckoning came, the master forgave the multi-million-dollar debtor every last penny. Instead of being overwhelmed with gratitude, however, the man who was forgiven much tracked down the man who owed him little, grabbed him by the throat, and dragged him away to debtors' prison. When the master heard all that had happened, his condemnation was swift and severe. The ungrateful servant was thrown into jail to be tortured until he could repay his debt in full—never!

When Jesus finished telling the story, he turned to his disciples and said, "This is how my heavenly Father will treat each of you unless you forgive your brother from your heart" (Matthew 18:35). The disciples immediately got the point. The debts we owe one another are like mere twenty-dollar bills compared to the infinite debt we owe our heavenly Father. Since we have been forgiven an infinite debt, it is a horrendous evil to even consider withholding forgiveness from those who seek it. If, for even a moment, we might wonder whether or not to forgive our debtors, this parable should immediately soften out hearts and illumine the darkness of our minds.

Furthermore, when we pray, "Forgive us our debts, as we also have forgiven our debtors," we are reminded of the infinite price that was paid so that we might be forgiven. We must ever be mindful that it was God himself who hung on the cross so that we could be reconciled to him for time and for eternity.

Multitudes have lost touch with this essential truth because they have little concept of the depravity of the human heart. As one postmodern American remarked, "The day I die, I should only have to look up at my Maker and say, 'Take me.' Not 'Forgive me.'"[1] Karl Menninger once lamented that we live in an I'm-OK-you're-OK world. In *Whatever Became of Sin?* he compares OK-ness in the face of human depravity to a bluebird on a dung heap.[2] The antidote to OK-ness is brokenness. And brokenness is the road map by which we find our way back to an intimate relationship with God.

King David is the quintessential example of such brokenness. After the prophet Nathan confronted him with his sin, he cried out,

Have mercy on me, O God,
  according to your unfailing love;
according to your great compassion
  blot out my transgressions.
Wash away all my iniquity
  and cleanse me from my sin.

For I know my transgressions,
  and my sin is always before me.
Against you, you only, have I sinned
  and done what is evil in your sight,
so that you are proven right when you speak
  and justified when you judge.
  (Psalm 51: 1–4)

Finally, I am reminded of what can happen when the prayer, "Forgive us our debts, as we also have forgiven our debtors," becomes a transforming power in our everyday lives. After watching the video of Christina receiving the Compassion Award, I had immersed myself in writing about forgiveness with renewed vigor and stamina. Time flew by. I glanced at my watch and suddenly realized that it was already well past midnight. I made some last-minute adjustments to my manuscript and headed for home.

I slipped quietly up the stairs and tiptoed into our bedroom.

"Hi, honey," came Kathy's voice out of the dark. As I bent over to give her a hug, she whispered in my ear, "Forgiveness really changes things."

"How so?" I asked. I heard the sheets rustle as Kathy reached over and turned on the light on the nightstand. In the soft glow I could see her eyes were wet with tears. She handed me a beautiful note etched in a child's handwriting. Below a smiley face in the shape of a heart I read these words:

DEAR Christna will you forgive me
I want to be your best
friend.
Love
KELSEY

If only we could learn to forgive and seek to be forgiven as quickly as children, I thought, as I got ready for bed.

As I slipped between the covers, I noticed that we were

The debts we owe one another are like mere twenty-dollar bills compared to the infinite debt we owe our heavenly Father.

not alone. My four-year-old daughter Faith lay curled up next to her mom. As I kissed her forehead, her eyes fluttered open. She reached out and put her little hands on my face, as she whispered, "You are the bestest daddy in the whole wide world."

"I don't feel like the best dad in the world today," I whispered back. "I forgot something very important."

"I know," she replied pertly, "but Christina forgives you."

I found it odd to hear the word "forgive" come out of my four-year-old's mouth, until I remembered that she, too, had been to her sister's award ceremony.

"Forgive? What does forgive mean?" I asked.

"It means that when you say you are sorry, you're supposed to say 'That's all right' and never think about it again."

I shook my head in astonishment. *"Out of the mouths of babes."*

Chapter Eight

The Armor

And lead us not into temptation,
but deliver us from the evil one.
—Matthew 6:13

My Dear Jezebelzebub:

I am commissioning you for the assignment of a generation. I have considered my legions of doom and have identified you as the very devil who can best pull it off. Even your name—derived from the best in human and demonic corruption—suggests that you have fallen for just such a time as this. Ah, even now the thought of Jezebel, who so admired my Beelzebubian ways, causes pride to rise up within the caldron of my nefarious mind.

Your mission—and you have no choice but to accept it—is to make sure the present generation of putrid evangelicals completely loses sight of the spiritual weapons of warfare listed in their manual under *the full armor of God.*

Perhaps a little history lesson will ignite the passions of your vile spirit and send you off on your assignment with malice and malevolence. I need not wax eloquent on the unfathomable pride that got me kicked out of the Adversary's presence. There are, however, some devilishly delicious lessons that you must glean from my award-winning performance in the garden.

Those goody two-shoes never even saw me coming. I was dressed in my satin best as I slithered up to Eve. Therein, of course, lies a scrumptious satanic secret— never let the maggots see you in your naked deformity! Always put your best falsehood forward. But I digress.

Remember my seductive line? *"You will be like God."* Not even I had any idea how hard and fast Eve would fall. A couple of bites later, she and that minnow-brained husband of hers were terminal. Just the thought of it makes my pride-pricked heart tingle with wicked delirium. Well, enough about me.

You, my dear Jezebelzebub, were not quite as successful with David. Remember the day he fell for Bathsheba? You thought you had won the war, but you only won a battle. If only you could have kept him from uttering that wretched prayer of confession. Even now the very thought of it makes me want to vomit. Like a pinhead you began celebrating before the game was even over. Thank hell, I was shrewd enough to discover another chink in David's armor.

I shall never forget the day I incited that little shepherd-boy-turned-king into taking a census. As any dog-eared-Bible reader will tell you, that was one of my greatest victories. Sensuality was a step in the right direction, but that census was a giant leap forward. The same slingshot boy who once cried out, "Who is that uncircumcised Philistine that he should defy the armies of the living God?" had begun to think those armies were his own doing. Pride, the mother of all other sins, had begun to brew like poison in his noxious little heart. He had fallen for the refrain of the damned—*me, my, mine.*

I was not quite as fortunate with the Root and the Offspring of David—the one they call the Second Adam. Remember those infamous wilderness temptations?

I looked for the soft underbelly. He was hungry, so I thought for sure he would fall for the change-the-stones-into-bread routine. When that failed, I quoted a sentence from an Old Testament passage and contextualized it with a seductive suggestion. But alas, the Carpenter's Son knew the Scriptures too well. So I moved with blinding speed to my fall-back position— the shortcut. "Forget that long, hard road to the cross," I purred. "Just make one short bow to me, and the kingdoms of this world will be yours." With anyone else it would have worked!

I bring up what you smart-mouthed, little minions refer to as "Beelzebub's boondoggle" for one hellish reason—to remind you that, whenever someone puts on the armor of the Adversary, we lose. When they don't, *we win.*

The first two human slugs dropped *the belt of truth* the moment they fell. Before the juice had even dried on her lips, Eve was already reciting the devil-made-me-do-it mantra. It didn't take long for *the breastplate of righteousness* to fall below David's knees either. Talk about a reproach to the *gospel of peace!* The moment he dropped *the shield of faith,* I knew he was no longer equipped to extinguish my flaming arrows. In fact, if David had not donned *the helmet of salvation* and prayed, "Restore to me the joy of your salvation," he would have been history.

The real danger, however, lies in the offensive weapons the Carpenter's Son wielded against me: *The sword of the Spirit and prayer.* It is imperative that today's generation be blinded to his example. And that, my dear Jezebelzebub, is precisely where you come in. Your expertise in the misuse of Scripture is notorious. Now I am counting on you to twist the very perception and practice of prayer. None of that *"Thy* name, *Thy* will, *Thy* kingdom" stuff. Your mission is to make selfish praying spiritual.

And let me forewarn you, if you should fail in your mission, there will be heaven to pay.

> Your superior in deceit,
> Lord Beelzebub

The moment I turned my attention to the final petition of the prayer of Jesus, I was moved to write the above

We must not expect that a man, unaided from above, should ever be a match for an angel, especially an angel whose intellect has been sharpened by malice.

fictional letter from Beelzebub to a demon named Jezebelzebub. I did so in part because I fear that we often underestimate the unmitigated hatred the Devil and his demons have for the things of God.

Therefore, when you pray, "Lead us not into temptation, but deliver us from the evil one," you should immediately remember to "put on the full armor of God so that you can take your stand against the devil's schemes." That, of course, means that you are not only intimately acquainted with each piece of the armor described by Paul in Ephesians 6, but you understand what each piece represents:

Stand firm then, with the belt of truth buckled around your waist, with the breastplate of righteousness in place, and with your feet fitted with the readiness that comes from the gospel of peace. In addition to all this, take up the shield of faith, with which you can extinguish all the flaming arrows of the evil one. Take the helmet of salvation and the sword of the Spirit, which is the word of God. And pray in the Spirit on all occasions with all kinds of prayers and requests. With this in mind, be alert and always keep on praying for all the saints. (vv. 14–18)

We must neither overestimate nor underestimate the power and province of our adversary. No doubt much to his delight, we often depict the Devil as the author of darkness in much the same way that God is described as the Author of Light. That, however, is far from true. God is the sovereign Author of all creation; Satan is but an angel that he has created. Satan is not the opposite of the Creator. Rather, as a fallen angel, he is the counterpart to the archangel Michael.

While it has become fashionable to credit the Devil with every temptation we face, we must be ever mindful that spiritual warfare involves the world and the flesh as well. As Jesus makes clear in the parable of the Sower, we are often fruitless because of "the worries of this life, and the deceitfulness of wealth" (Matthew 13:22).

Just as we should never overestimate the Devil, we would also err greatly in underestimating his cunning craftiness. He is a malevolent being, the vastness of whose intellect exceeds that of any human who has ever lived from Solomon to Socrates. Thus, "we must not expect that a man, unaided from above, should ever be a match for an angel, especially an angel whose intellect has been sharpened by malice."[1] From the primordial garden to the present generation, he and his hellish hordes have honed the craft of temptation. He knew just what to say to tempt Eve to fall into a life of constant sin terminated by death. And twice, the tempter found David's Achilles' heel and sent flaming arrows deep into his soul.

Furthermore, when we pray "lead us not into temptation, but deliver us from the evil one," we are acknowledging that God is sovereign over all things, including the temptations of Satan. Augustine rightly referred to the evil one as "the ape of God." Likewise, Luther called the devil "God's devil." While our "enemy the devil prowls around like a roaring lion looking for someone to devour" (1 Peter 5:8), he is a lion on a leash the length of which is determined by the Lord.

It is significant to note that Jesus was "led *by the Spirit* into the desert to be tempted by the devil" (Matthew 4:1). Thus, while Satan was the *agent of the temptation,* God was *the author of the testing.* Satan used the occasion to tempt Christ to sin; God used the occasion to demonstrate that he could not sin.

Finally, whenever we pray "lead us not into temptation, but deliver us from the evil one," we are reminded to look forward to the day when we will be completely set free from all temptations. The very fact that Jesus withstood the temptations in the wilderness is our guarantee that one day soon the Kingdom will be ours. The tempter will be thrown into the lake of burning sulfur (Revelation 20:10), and temptations, such as those depicted in the letter above, will be no more. We will enter the golden City with divine assurance that "nothing impure will ever enter it, nor will anyone who does what is shameful or deceitful, but only those whose names are written in the Lamb's book of life" (Revelation 21:27).

Chapter Nine

Into the Deep

As the deer pants for streams of water,
so my soul pants for you, O God.
—Psalm 42:1

I will never forget the day she read me the story. I was in pain and could hardly move. Sensing that she had a captive audience, my wife pulled up a chair next to the shallow waters of the tub in which I was soaking and began to read from a book titled *Into the Depths of God*.[1] The words were both refreshing and riveting. They washed over me like the balm of Gilead. Within moments I became oblivious to my pain.

This was not the stuff of shallow men who splash around in surface things and attempt to write about the deep. It was not the stuff of "non-peakers talking to non-peakers about peak experiences."[2] These were the words of someone who had escaped the shallowness of his own soul and plunged deep into the ocean of God's immensity.

As Kathy read, I was brought into the experience of the author and his family as they traveled to the Great Barrier Reef. Calvin Miller had come to snorkel in the shallow waters above the reef. His son had come to scuba. For the rest of their lives both father and son would tell stories of their experiences with the Great Reef. Only one of them, however, had *really* come to know it.

How appropriate an analogy for prayer. Most men snorkel in the surface waters of prayer and succeed only in sunburning their backs. They fail to comprehend that "deep is where the noisy, trashy surface of the ocean gets quiet and serene."[3] It is where our noisy requests give way to the quiet of a relationship with our Maker. The tragedy, says Miller, is that most believers "spend their lives being whipped tumultuously through the surface circumstances of their days. Their frothy lifestyles mark the surface nature of their lives. Yet those who plumb the deep things of God discover true peace for the first time."[4]

Deep is where we step out of the shallow tidepool of our hearts into the boundless ocean of God's power and presence. It is where we get beyond surface things and plunge into a deep relationship with our Creator. Jesus wanted his disciples to venture out of the

Relationships, whether human or divine, never grow apart from the investment of quality time.

shallow waters of prayer. Thus, when they began begging him to teach them to pray, he offered the pattern of his own personal prayer life as a brilliant shaft leading deep into the ocean of prayer. Scuba gear allowed Miller's son to have a real experience with the Great Reef. The prayer of Jesus is the entryway into an ever-deepening experience with God.

THE SHIFT

Going deep with God begins with a major paradigm shift in our perceptions about prayer. Rather than looking for techniques through which we can get God to answer our prayers, we must be ever mindful that prayer is an opportunity for developing intimacy with the very One who knit us together in our mother's womb. That, of course, is precisely why the prayer of Jesus begins by modeling how we are to build a relationship with our heavenly Father before it instructs us on how to bring him our requests.

If we are honest with ourselves, most of us have learned to pray backwards. We hurry into God's presence with a laundry list of prayer requests. And before our knees have even touched the ground we are already thinking about getting back to our frenzied lifestyles. Often we treat our heavenly Father no better than we treat our families. We want a relationship without the discipline of investing quality time. I can assure you that Kathy would not be flattered by a request from me for physical intimacy devoid of a relationship. Likewise, God is not flattered when we bring him our requests without building our relationships.

The bottom line is this: Relationships, whether human or divine, never grow apart from the investment of quality time. Thus, the first step toward moving into the deep with God is to purpose to make prayer a priority.

THE SOUNDS OF SILENCE

Think for a moment about your prayer life. Could it be that it is characterized by constant babbling? Might it be that even the chatter of your mind is deafening? Could it be that your shallow askings drown out the sound of the very One whose voice you so long to hear? Have you ever considered how glorious the sounds of silence might be?

If not, I encourage you to develop the discipline of listening for the voice of God. Three times God called out to Samuel. But Samuel did not recognize his voice. It was not until God spoke the fourth time that Samuel said, *"Speak,* for your servant is *listening"* (1 Samuel 3:10).

The Bible never encourages us to stamp out the self as the Buddhists do. It does, however, exhort us to stamp out the selfishness. Genuine prayer is not found in our noisy askings and gettings; it is found in a growing relationship with the Lover of our souls. All too often we want God to move the fence posts and enlarge our houses and lands. God wants something far better for us. He wants us to be still so that he can enlarge the territories of

The more you meditate on Scripture, the clearer the voice of the Master will be within the sounds of silence.

our hearts. He has sent us sixty-six love letters etched in heavenly handwriting. And the more we meditate upon those words, the clearer his voice will resonate in the sounds of our silence.

I have learned more about prayer from my wife's example than from anything I have ever read in a book. Just last night Kathy shared an example of hearing God's voice in the sounds of silence. It was a letter that she had written to some friends who had lost their precious daughter. After pouring out her heart to the Lord, she fell silent in the comforting presence of her heavenly Father. Sometime within the sounds of silence she heard God speak. Kathy knew the words were not meant for her ears alone. And so she began to write.

Last night as I read those words I recognized the unmistakable voice of the Master. I knew that my wife had not merely snorkeled in shallow tidepools but had plunged deeply into God's Word.

Make no mistake about it. Kathy is no modern-day

prophet. Instead, she had taken another step into the deep—hiding God's Word in her heart. The more you meditate on Scripture, the clearer the voice of the Master will be within the sounds of silence.

THE SECRET PLACE

I conclude by exploring one final step into the deep. When Kathy poured out her heart to the Lord, she did so in the secret place. Early in the morning she had slipped off to the secret place to be alone with God. Our ultimate example, of course, is Jesus. Scripture tells us that often he "withdrew to lonely places and prayed" (Luke 5:16). Christ longed to be alone with his Father in the secret place.

Do you have a secret place? A place where you can drown out the static of the world and hear the voice of your heavenly Father? Kathy's place is the sauna. Mine is walking.

The issue, of course, is not location but motivation. We are all unique creations of God. Thus, your secret place will no doubt be different than mine. The point is that we desperately need a place away from the invasive sounds of this world so that we can hear the sounds of another place and another voice. Do you hear it? You will if you yearn for it with all your heart

In the quiet words of the hymn, "I Come to the Garden Alone," writer Austin Miles says it beautifully:

He speaks, and the sound of his voice is so sweet
The birds hush their singing.
And the melody that he gave to me
Within my heart is ringing.

And he walks with me, and he talks with me,
And he tells me I am his own,
And the joy we share as we tarry there,
None other has ever known.[5]

Chapter Ten

Embracing the Prayer of Jesus

"Therefore everyone who hears these words of mine
and puts them into practice is like a wise man . . ."
—Matthew 7:24

I want to let you in on a secret. But you've got to promise not to tell anyone. You see, I'm a golf addict. I might as well come right out and say it, *"I love Golf!"* If there were such a thing as Golfers Anonymous, I would have enrolled in it years ago. For the better part of forty years I have worked hard at mastering the game I love. In the process I have fallen for my share of faddish formulas that promised a better golf life in thirty days or your money back.

I vividly remember falling hard for a book that promised to "redefine how we play." The book promised, "rewards would come quickly" and offered a seemingly endless stream of accessories from training aids to tee shirts. All I had to do was begin thinking about golf in a new and better way.

To top it all off, the book had fallen into my hands at just the right moment. Or so I thought. In less than a month I would be playing in a Pro-Am that precedes a nationally televised golf tournament called The Skins Game. The four contestants that year were Fred Couples, John Daly, Tom Watson, and Tiger Woods. It was reported that the tournament turned out to be one of the highest rated golf shows in national television history. Needless to say, I desperately wanted to be in peak form.

During the month before the tournament, I followed the "proven techniques" to a tee and seemed to experience some amazing results. I even watched an infomercial laced with convincing testimonials from people whose golfing lives had been revolutionized. The credibility of the spokesman was impeccable. He was an accomplished golfer who essentially promised that this easy-to-remember formula had been the key to his success. I became so convinced that I had finally found "the secret" that I passed the book around to several of my very best golf friends.

At the dinner reception after the Pro-Am I decided to ask Tiger what he thought about "the secret." His reaction was classic. Before he even opened his mouth, the answer was obvious. Rather than taking Tiger's unspoken warning, I resolved to prove him wrong. I can still remember thinking, *What does he know?* (In my defense, this was 1996, long before he had become the most recognizable athlete on the planet.)

In time, however, I experienced what every player has who has fallen for a fad experience. Discouragement and disillusionment. Unless you have been living in a cave, you know exactly what I am talking about. You may never have fallen for a newfangled faddish golf formula, but perhaps you have fallen just as hard for something else. Maybe it was the secret to a successful marriage, the secret to beating the stock market, or the secret to losing thirty pounds in thirty days. The list is endless.

I bring this up because I want to make you a promise: The prayer of Jesus is not a passing fancy. When Peter and the disciples expectantly begged Jesus for bread, he did not give them a stone.

I have had the experience eight times now, and every time it was a struggle. As my children began to outgrow their diapers, I would try to talk them into leaving the kiddie pool and launching out into the deep. For them the kiddie pool was all there was and ever would be. That is, of course, until they experienced the deep. Once they learned how to swim in the ocean, they forever lost their appetite for shallow water.

As I led each one of my children into an experience with the vastness of the ocean, so too Jesus led his disciples out of the shallow tidepools of prayer into an ever deepening relationship with their heavenly Father.

Here are some practical guidelines for diving in.

One—Make the paradigm shift. Stop seeing prayer as merely a means of obtaining your requests. Start seeing prayer as a means of enjoying the riches of a relationship with God. In other words, learn well the F-A-C-T-S on prayer presented in Chapter Three.

Two—Confess your sins daily. Every single prayer, including the prayer of Jesus, will bounce right off the ceiling if there is unforgiveness in your heart, which is precisely why Jesus ended his public sermon on prayer with these words: "For if you forgive men when they sin against you, your heavenly Father will also forgive you. But if you do not forgive men their sins, your Father will not forgive your sins" (Matthew 6:14–15).

Three—Get into the Bible. God's will is revealed in his Word. Thus the only way you can know his will is to know his Word. The more we meditate upon God's Word, the clearer his voice will be as we daily commune with him in prayer.

Four—Discover your secret place. The secret to prayer is secret prayer. Your public presence is a direct reflection of your private prayer life. If you spend time in the secret place, you will exude peace in the midst of life's storms. If you do not, you will be a poster child for Busy-anity rather than Christianity.

Five—Make prayer a priority. Wisdom is the application of knowledge. As the Master put it, "Therefore everyone who hears these words of mine and puts them into practice [or applies them] is like a wise man who built his house on the rock (Matthew 7:24)." My experience in teaching memory for over two decades demonstrates that, if you faithfully practice a new discipline for twenty-one days, it may well stay with you for the rest of your life.

THE MOMENT OF TRUTH

After my encounter with Tiger Woods at the Skins Game, my golf swing continued to deteriorate. The moment of truth arrived when I went back to an old friend who had worked with me over the years on the fundamentals of golf. God had used me to lead him to faith in Christ. Now he was giving me a lesson.

He watched me take a few swings and knew immediately what the problem was. "Hank," he said choosing his words carefully, "you love golf far too much to ever take another shortcut." Over the next few hours, Fred patiently reacquainted me with the basics. I was amazed at how quickly things fell back into place. Within weeks I was playing the best golf of my life.

As much as I love golf, I love God infinitely more. Golf is a hobby. God is my life. It stands to reason, therefore, that I would put a whole lot more time and effort into learning the principles of praying than learning the principles of playing.

Prayer is a beautiful foretaste of something we will experience for all eternity. Paradise lost will soon become Paradise restored and a whole lot more. For we will experience something not even Adam and Eve experienced— face-to-face communication with the very One who taught us the prayer of Jesus.

Our Father in heaven,
hallowed be your name,
your kingdom come,
your will be done
on earth as it is in heaven.
Give us today our daily bread.
Forgive us our debts,
as we also have forgiven our debtors.
And lead us not into temptation,
but deliver us from the evil one,
for yours is the kingdom
and the power and the glory forever.
Amen.

(Matthew 6:9–13, NIV)

Endnotes

Introduction

1. For April 5, 2001, *The Prayer of Jabez* (Sisters, Ore.: Multnomah Press, 2001) by Bruce H. Wilkinson with David Kopp was number 3 on the *USA Today* Bestsellers list ahead of J. K. Rowling's *Harry Potter and the Sorcerer's Stone* (New York: Scholastic Press, 1998), which was number 7. During the week of April 22, *The Prayer of Jabez* reached first on the New York *Times* Advice, How-to & Miscellaneous bestseller list, its seventh week on that list, despite the fact that the *Times* does not count books sold through religious bookstores. Also, during March, *The Prayer of Jabez* was number 1 on *Publishers Weekly* Religion Bestsellers Hardcover list and for a time in April was the number 1 seller at Amazon.com. With 3.5 million copies sold as of April, *Publishers Weekly* religion editor Lynn Garrett comments, "[*The Prayer of Jabez*] could easily become this year's hardcover bestseller" (quoted in David Van Biema, "A Prayer with Wings," *Time;* 23 April 2001, 76).
2. Bruce H. Wilkinson with David Kopp, *The Prayer of Jabez.*
3. Quoted in David Van Biema, "A Prayer with Wings," *Time,* 23 April 2001, 76.
4. Ibid.

Chapter 1: Lord Teach Us Now to Pray

1. The Greek word that is translated "teach" is an aorist imperative, which may imply a slight sense of urgency: "teach us now to pray" (see Darrell L. Bock, *Luke Volume 2: Baker Exegetical*

Commentary on the New Testament [Grand Rapids, Mich.: Baker Books, 1996], 1050).

Chapter 2: The Secret
1. Bill Plaschke, "Master of All," *Los Angeles Times*, 9 April 2001, D10.
2. Philip Graham Ryken, *When You Pray* (Wheaton, Ill.: Crossway Books, 2000), 21.
3. Calvin Miller, *Into the Depths of God* (Minneapolis, Minn.: Bethany House Publishers, 2000), 29.
4. Ibid., 30.
5. Ibid., 32.
6. Emilie Griffin, *Clinging* (New York: McCracken Press, 1984), 15; as quoted in Calvin Miller, *Into the Depths of God,* 32.

Chapter 3: Your Father Knows
1. Paul Overstreet and Don Schlitz, "I Won't Take Less Than Your Love," (Pegram, Tenn.: Scarlet Moon Records, 1999).
2. F-A-C-T-S discussion adapted from Hank Hanegraaff, *Christianity in Crisis* (Eugene Ore.: Harvest House Publishers, 1997), 288–90; A-C-T-S used widely many years.
3. R. A. Torrey, *The Power of Prayer* (Grand Rapids, Mich.: Zondervan, 1981), 123–24, emphasis in original.
4. Shakespeare, *Macbeth*, V, I, 34–57.
5. C. S. Lewis, *God in the Dock,* edited by William Hooper (Wm. B. Eerdmans Pub. Co., 1970, 1979 repr.), 105.
6. Ibid., 105–06.
7. Ibid., 107.

Chapter 4: Building Our Relationship
1. For another version of this joke, see Michael Youssef's excellent book, *The Prayer That God Answers* (Nashville: Thomas Nelson, 2000), 8.

2. Philip Graham Ryken, *When You Pray* (Wheaton, Ill.: Crossway Books, 2000), 46.
3. Ibid., 48.
4. I am deeply indebted to Philip Graham Ryken for his insight on this matter.
5. Dr. Adolph Saphir, as quoted in Philip Graham Ryken, *When You Pray* (Wheaton, Ill.: Crossway Books, 2000), 9.
6. Saint Augustine, *Our Lord's Sermon on the Mount*, II:V, in Philip Schaff, ed., *The Nicene and Post-Nicene Fathers, First Series,* vol. VI (Grand Rapids: William B. Eerdmans Publishing Co., reprinted 1980), 40; also quoted in part in Philip Graham Ryken, *When You Pray,* 70.
7. R. C. Sproul, *Effective Prayer* (Wheaton, Ill.: Tyndale House Publishers, 1984), 31.
8. Philip Graham Ryken, *When You Pray,* 75.

Chapter 5: The City of God

1. Philip Graham Ryken, *When You Pray* (Wheaton, Ill.: Crossway Books, 2000), 78.
2. C. S. Lewis, *Mere Christianity* (New York: Collier Books, 1960), 36.
3. Anthony A. Hoekema, *The Bible and the Future* (Grand Rapids, Mich.: William B. Eerdmans Publishing Co., 1979), 21.
4. Ibid., 31.
5. Gordon D. Fee, *The Disease of the Health and Wealth Gospels* (Somerville, Mass.: Frontline Publishing, 1985), 22.
6. Darrel W. Amundsen, "The Anguish and Agonies of Charles Spurgeon," *Christian History* 10, 1 (1991): 22–25 at 25b–c.
7. R. C. Sproul, *Effective Prayer* (Wheaton, Ill.: Tyndale House Publishers, 1984), 34.
8. Philip Graham Ryken, *When You Pray,* 92.
9. Tertullian, *On Prayer,* VI, in Alexander Roberts and James

Donaldson, eds, *The Ante-Nicene Fathers,* vol. III (Grand Rapids: William B. Eerdmans Publishing Co., reprinted in 1986), 683; also quoted in Philip Graham Ryken, *When You Pray,* 105.

Chapter 6: Bringing Our Requests
1. Martin Chemnitz, *The Lord's Prayer* (St. Louis: Concordia Publishing House, 1999), 57.
2. Ibid., 58.
3. R. C. Sproul, *Effective Prayer* (Wheaton, Ill.: Tyndale House Publishers, 1984), 34.
4. Philip Graham Ryken, *When You Pray* (Wheaton, Ill.: Crossway Books, 2000), 115–16.

Chapter 7: The Compassion Award
1. Quoted in Marianne Meye Thompson, *1–3 John* (Downers Grove, Ill.: InterVarsity Press, 1992), 46.
2. Calvin Miller, *Into the Depths of God* (Minneapolis, Minn.: Bethany House Publishers, 2000), 179.

Chapter 8: The Armor
1. Charles Spurgeon, compiled and edited by Robert Hall, *Spiritual Warfare in a Believer's Life* (Lynwood, Wash.: Emerald Books, 1993), 30.

Chapter 9: Into the Deep
1. Calvin Miller, *Into the Depths of God* (Minneapolis, Minn.: Bethany House Publishers, 2000), 179.
2. Ibid., 179.
3. Ibid., 180.
4. Ibid., 180.
5. C. Austin Miles, "I Come to the Garden Alone," (1912).

THE PRAYER OF JESUS
STUDY GUIDE

LESSON ONE: Lord, Teach Us Now to Pray

"One day Jesus was praying in a certain place. When he finished, one of his disciples said to him, 'Lord, teach us to pray, just as John taught his disciples.'" (Luke 11:1)

Reflect for a moment on your prayer life. Then meditate for a few moments on Matthew 6:9–13. What misconceptions do you think you have had about prayer?

_____

_____

_____

_____

Write down your working definition of prayer.

_____

_____

_____

_____

"Jesus knew that his disciples would never properly understand examples of prayer without first understanding principles of prayer. And that's exactly why he gave us the prayer of Jesus. He did not give us a prayer mantra; he gave us a prayer pattern."

—HANK HANEGRAAFF

Fleshing out our Lord's concise teaching on the principles of prayer is what Hank's book *The Prayer of Jesus* is all about. Before diving in to the rest of this study, try to identify and list some of the principles Jesus had in mind. (See Matthew 6:5–15.)

_____

_____

_____

_____

_____

_____

_____

Prayer Journal:

"Teach me your way, O LORD, and I will walk in your truth; give me an undivided heart, that I may fear your name." (Psalm 86:11)

There are many kinds of studies on prayer, and you may have been involved in a Bible study centered on this discipline before. One thing you may have concluded is that it is a lot easier to talk about prayer than to actually do it.

Prayer is not merely a means of presenting our requests, it is a means of pursuing a dynamic relationship with our heavenly Father. As you write out your prayers, ask God to teach you his ways as you pray. Take time to listen for his voice to instruct you. Share with the Lord which aspects of prayer are difficult for you.

Lord, teach me to pray. I humbly come to you, my Teacher, to learn from your example . . .

_____

_____

_____

_____

_____

LESSON TWO: The Secret

"But when you pray, go into your room, close the door and pray to your Father, who is unseen. Then your Father, who sees what is done in secret, will reward you." (Matthew 6:6)

Do you find it more difficult to pray alone or in groups? Why do you think this is the case?

_____

_____

_____

_____

In Mathew 6:6, Jesus was not opposing corporate prayer. This, too, is an important aspect of our prayer lives. But Jesus did warn us that prayer should not be done for the approval of men. Motives are very important to God. Reflect on how your private prayer life differs from your public prayer life. Describe some of your frustrations with your personal prayer life. Then think of some ways to confront this problem.

Hank mentions, "The tragedy of contemporary Christianity is that we measure the success of our prayer life by the size and scope of our accomplishments, rather than the strength of our relationships with God." Do you think this is true for you? How do you personally measure the success of your prayer life?

_____

_____

_____

_____

_____

"The secret to prayer is secret prayer."

—HANK HANEGRAAFF

Hank uses the example of Tiger Woods to illustrate the point that the best way to improve prayer is to practice—to just *do* it. Prayer is not a spectator sport. Furthermore, we practice when no one is looking. If the practice is genuine, then at a certain point of development, the watching world doesn't matter anymore. Like a skilled player who doesn't listen to the crowd, a mature "pray-er" carries on in public as he does in private. Prayer is hard work, and we must practice this discipline daily.

List some of the hindrances in your life that keep you from giving God quality communion with you in prayer. What are some practical steps you can take to remove at least one of these hindrances this week?

_____

_____

_____

_____

_____

_____

_____

_____

Many modern-day athletes struggle with addictions. But the truth is, many Christians struggle with other addictions that aren't as obvious as substance abuse. What consuming appetites do you think you might be battling?

_____

_____

_____

_____

_____

_____

_____

"Jesus often withdrew to lonely places and prayed" (Luke 5:16). Write down a lonely place you can go to pray. Is this a place where you can enter into prayer without distractions? Do you find it difficult to be completely alone with God?

_____

_____

_____

_____

_____

Prayer Journal:

Hank writes, "If we are honest with ourselves, most of us have learned to pray backwards. We hurry into God's presence with a laundry list of prayer requests. And before our knees have even touched the ground, we are already thinking about getting back to our frenzied lifestyles." Many Christians are addicted to busyness. We can fill our calendar with "good" things, but God may be calling you to learn about resting in him. Prayer is not a magic formula that allows us to get through a list of tasks for the day. Communing with God in prayer is itself the prize.

Father, help me to experience ever more fully the blessing of resting in your presence through the finished work of Jesus Christ. Show me how to . . .

_____

_____

_____

_____

_____

"Let us draw near to God with a sincere heart in full assurance of faith." (Hebrews 10:22)

LESSON THREE: Your Father Knows

"And when you pray, do not keep on babbling like pagans,
for they think they will be heard because of their many words.
Do not be like them, for your Father knows what you need
before you ask him." (Matthew 6:7–8)

F-A-C-T-S PRAYER GUIDE

We have been conditioned to think that supplication is the sole sum
and substance of prayer. Genuine prayer, however, is not found in our
noisy askings and gettings; it is found in a growing relationship with the
Lover of our souls. Hank uses his adaptation of a well-known acronym
to introduce some of the essential elements of prayer that go beyond
mere asking and getting and enhance our relationship of loving intimacy with our heavenly Father. The following exercises will help you
understand and remember these elements, all of which are either
explicitly or implicitly included in the pattern of the Lord's Prayer.

FAITH:

Our faith is built up by reading God's Word. Sometimes we feel
as if we have to conjure up belief, but that is only faith in our *faith*,
not true faith in God. Romans 10:17 says, "Faith comes from hearing
the message, and the message is heard through the word of Christ."

How would you rate your faith in God right now, on a scale of 1
to 10? Take a moment to find some passages in Scripture that talk
about faith (for example, Matthew 6:25–34; Romans 4; Hebrews 11;
James 1:2–8). Read them and write down any new thoughts you
gain about faith.

_____

_____

_____

Prayer Journal:

When life isn't going the way we hoped, it is easy for the Word of God to be snatched from our hearts. We can forget his promises of faithfulness, take our eyes off of God, and focus on ourselves. If this sounds like you, lift your eyes to heaven—right now—and express your faith in God through prayer.

Lord, I believe that you are powerful to accomplish your will in and through our lives. Please help me to understand your Word and to trust in your faithfulness. Help me to believe that . . .

_____

_____

_____

_____

_____

_____

_____

ADORATION:

"Faith in God naturally leads to adoration."
—HANK HANEGRAAFF

Through the act of adoration, we express our genuine, heartfelt love and longing for God. Adoration inevitably leads to praise and worship. When we focus on God's surpassing greatness, we can better see our need for him.

What are some expressions of adoration that you can say to God today?

_____

_____

_____

_____

Why do you think God merits all of our adoration? Reflect a bit on the meaning of adoration and write out your thoughts.

_____

_____

_____

_____

Now read Psalm 145. David adored God so much that he could not contain his adoration and worship. What are some of God's praiseworthy attributes for which David adored and praised him?

_____

_____

_____

_____

Compare your reasons for adoring God with David's. How often do you spend time thinking about the attributes of God mentioned in this psalm? Make it your goal to read and meditate on Psalm 145 every day for the next week so that by thinking of God as David did you might develop the type of adoration for God that leads to a lifestyle of genuine worship and praise.

Prayer Journal:

Lord, I adore you. You are alone God. You are able to do more than we ask, think, or imagine. You deserve all my praise because . . .

_____

_____

_____

_____

_____

_____

CONFESSION:

Another important aspect of prayer is confession. Though we know we live as forgiven people because of Christ's gift of salvation, unconfessed sin affects how we relate to God. Jesus did not want his disciples to live under the bondage of sin and guilt. He knew that unconfessed sin would harm our relationship with him. When we know we have sinned, often our natural inclination is to hide from him, just as Adam and Eve did in the Garden of Eden.

Write out some sins that you need to confess to the Lord. You may also wish to determine if you have sinned against someone and if you need to ask for his or her forgiveness as well. Be honest with the Lord, and he will be faithful to show his mercy and love to you in a new way.

_____

_____

_____

_____

Read Psalm 32. What does this psalm teach us about the importance of confessing sin? What other benefits of confessing sin to the Lord can you think of?

_____

_____

_____

_____

Prayer Journal:

Lord Jesus, I know that you are a forgiving God. I want to confess to you that I . . .

_____

_____

THANKSGIVING:

Do you struggle with ingratitude? Do you often compare your situation with those around you, finding yourself envious of those who appear to be more blessed than you? The apostle Paul says we are to "be joyful always; pray continually; give thanks in all circumstances, for this is God's will for you in Christ Jesus" (1 Thessalonians 5:16–18; see also Ephesians 5:20). Jesus knew that giving thanks to God would keep us from living out a life of ingratitude.

How does thanksgiving help us to overcome our tendency to forget what God has done for us? List five things you are thankful for that immediately come to your mind.

_____

_____

_____

_____

_____

_____

_____

_____

_____

Ask the Lord to reveal to you any hidden ungratefulness that you carry in your heart.

_____

_____

_____

_____

_____

_____

_____

Read Psalm 66 as an example of overflowing gratitude toward God. For what kinds of things was this psalmist thankful? How can meditating on this and other scriptural examples help you to maintain an attitude of thanksgiving to God?

_____

_____

_____

_____

Use the THANKGSGIVING acrostic below to create a list of people, events, and gifts for which you are thankful to God. List one item (or more) for each letter.

T

H

A

N

K

S

G

I

V

I

N

G

After this exercise, determine whether any attitudes changed in your heart.

_____

_____

_____

_____

_____

Prayer Journal:

Lord Jesus, thank you for . . .

_____

_____

_____

_____

_____

_____

_____

_____

_____

SUPPLICATION:

We must ever be mindful of the fact that the purpose of supplication is not to pressure God into providing us with provisions and pleasures, but rather to conform us to his purposes. While our Father knows what we need before we even ask, the act of supplication itself is an acknowledgment of our dependence on him. And that is only one reason why we should "pray without ceasing."

Do you find it difficult to ask God for things? Why or why not?

_____

_____

_____

_____

_____

_____

_____

_____

_____

Imagine if you found out that your child was hiding food from each meal in his room, for fear that you as a parent would not provide for his nourishment the next day. How would that make you feel? Think about how not trusting God dishonors him.

_____

_____

_____

_____

_____

_____

List some of your needs that are weighing down on you today. Which ones are harder to trust God for? Write down an answer to prayer you received during a particularly difficult time in your life. Take a moment to reflect on God's faithfulness in the past that is also available to you right now. (If you have not yet read Hebrews 11 as suggested above under the study on faith, do so now to see that we should trust God to fulfill his promises for the future based on his proven faithfulness in the past.)

_____

_____

_____

_____

_____

Prayer Journal:

Lord, you tell us to pray, "Give us this day our daily bread." I acknowledge that I need your strength and provision for . . .

_____

_____

_____

LESSON FOUR: Building Our Relationship

"Our Father in heaven, hallowed be your name." (Matthew 6:9)

Jesus made every word he spoke count. Jesus' prayer has the ability to take us where the Lord wants to take us in prayer. It is much more than just an incantation or vain repetition. This prayer can deepen our relationship with Christ and provide us with a better understanding of how great our God really is.

Why do you think Jesus made a point to talk about how to address God? What attributes does a Father have?

_____

_____

_____

_____

_____

_____

How does our culture contribute to a diminished view of God and an exalted view of man? Read Psalm 8 and find out how God views us.

_____

_____

_____

_____

_____

"[God's] dominion is an eternal dominion; his kingdom endures from generation to generation. All the peoples of the earth are regarded as nothing. He does as he pleases with the powers of heaven and the peoples of the earth. No one can hold back his hand or say to him: 'What have you done?'" (Daniel 4:34–35)

The initial petition of the prayer of Jesus is that God's name be revered because he is holy. To pray "hallowed be your name" is to put the emphasis on God first and to pray that:

- God be given the reverence his holiness demands;
- God's church be led by faithful pastors and preserved from pitfalls;
- We be kept from language that profanes God's name;
- Our thought lives remain holy.

Can you think of other ways that God's holiness is made known in and through the lives of his people?

_____
_____
_____
_____
_____
_____
_____
_____

List some of God's attributes that make him "Totally Other" and set apart. Reflect on the wonderful truth that the holy God of the universe condescended to dwell among us and allows us to be called his children, heirs of his kingdom.

_____
_____
_____
_____
_____
_____
_____

Prayer Journal:

Lord, today I magnify your name. You are holy and the Lord Almighty. Thank you for the privilege of knowing you as our Father. Teach me how to magnify your Name and . . .

_____

_____

_____

_____

_____

_____

_____

_____

_____

_____

_____

_____

_____

_____

_____

_____

_____

_____

_____

_____

_____

_____

_____

"Don't worry about having the right words; worry more about having the right heart. It's not eloquence He seeks, just honesty."

—Max Lucado

LESSON FIVE: The City of God

"Your kingdom come, your will be done on earth as it is in heaven." (Matthew 6:10)

In teaching us to pray, "your kingdom come," Jesus was first and foremost teaching us to petition our heavenly Father to expand his rule over the territory of our hearts. It is an invitation to embrace the kingdom of Christ in every aspect of our lives. Furthermore, Jesus wanted us to ask God to use our witness for the expansion of his kingdom. While we know we are caught between D-day and V-day, we are to ask God to reign here and now.

What parts of your life are you holding back from God? Do you feel he is reigning over all of your life?

_____

_____

_____

_____

Read Romans 12:2. Identify some ways that society has influenced you negatively. What "patterns of the world" are you currently trying to resist?

_____

_____

_____

_____

What are some memorable ways God has answered your prayers when you have wanted his reign and will, not your own?

_____

_____

_____

To ask, "your will be done on earth as it is in heaven," reminds us that there are still those in the world who rebel against his will and, as a result, we face trials and tribulations as the kingdom of God expands on earth. Continually seeking after the accomplishment of the Lord's will rather than our own is the only way to ensure that those inevitable trials will help us to become more like Christ. As we seek the Lord through his Word and prayer, he will give us not only the opportunity but the ability to join him in his work. Luke 10:2 says, "The harvest is plentiful, but the workers are few. Ask the Lord of the harvest, therefore, to send out workers into his harvest field."

Are there people within the sphere of your influence to whom the Holy Spirit is prompting you to testify through your life? If so, list one or more of these people below and begin to include them in your daily petitions.

_____

_____

_____

In a fallen world, sometimes it is easy to forget that Christ has already won the war, though his reign here on earth is not fully realized. How can acknowledging this truth change our outlook?

_____

_____

_____

Think of some past prayer requests that, looking back, you know would not have been best for you. How would your life be different if God had answered your request the way you wanted?

_____

_____

_____

_____

Prayer Journal:

Sometimes we are faced with not knowing what God's will is in a situation. Many times, words seem inadequate and we don't really even know what to say to God, as our own understanding can be very limited. Romans 8:26 reminds us that we are never facing prayer alone. The Holy Spirit is interceding for us: "In the same way, the Spirit helps us in our weakness. We do not know what we ought to pray for, but the Spirit himself intercedes for us with groans that words cannot express."

Father, thank you that you give me what is best for me, not always what I ask for. I surrender . . .

_____

_____

_____

_____

_____

_____

_____

_____

_____

_____

_____

_____

_____

_____

_____

"And we know that in all things God works for the good of those who love him, who have been called according to his purpose." (Romans 8:28)

LESSON SIX: Bringing Our Requests

"Give us today our daily bread." (Matthew 6:11)

Petitioning our heavenly Father to "give us today our daily bread" encompasses all things that are necessary to sustain our bodies and lives. In addition, we are also connected to the community of Christ as we ask for the needs of others. We do not pray as mere rugged individualists but as members of a community of faith.

The word *bread* in the context of the prayer of Jesus can be rightly understood in a larger sense to encompass all things necessary for the peaceable and honest ordering of our lives. Which of these necessities do you find yourself taking for granted?

_____

_____

_____

_____

_____

It is hard to pray "give" without being givers ourselves. Can you think of someone who needs your help today? Why not pray for that person right now—then take the next step and put feet to your faith! As a reminder, make a note below regarding whom you have purposed to help and what you have purposed to do.

_____

_____

_____

_____

"I tell you the truth, anyone who gives you a cup of water in my name because you belong to Christ will certainly not lose his reward." (Mark 9:41)

God promises to provide the necessities, but not always the niceties. What things are you asking for that you think God might be asking you to give up?

_____

_____

_____

_____

We know that God was not just talking about our physical needs being met in Matthew 6:11. He also promised to meet our spiritual needs. What spiritual needs do you feel you have right now? Have you asked the Lord specifically to meet these needs?

_____

_____

_____

_____

Prayer Journal:

When we come to the petition "Give us today our daily bread," we also should use this time in prayer to think of the needs of others in our lives. Think of someone in particular whom you are concerned about.

Lord, I thank you for this opportunity to pray for others, specifically for . . .

_____

_____

_____

_____

_____

_____

_____

_____

LESSON SEVEN: The Compassion Award

"Forgive us our debts, as we also have forgiven our debtors."
(Matthew 6:12)

One of the most riveting parables Jesus ever communicated to his disciples is found in Matthew 18:23–35. It is the story of two debtors and a master who truly deserved a "Compassion Award." Take time to read this story and let the Holy Spirit speak to you.

Are you truly mindful of the fact that you have been forgiven an infinite debt and that it is a horrendous evil to even consider withholding forgiveness from those who seek it? If not, ask the Lord to help you be willing to forgive anyone who sincerely seeks your forgiveness. Write out your thoughts about this below.

_____

_____

_____

_____

_____

_____

Have you grown indifferent to Jesus' sacrifice? Can you think of anyone you have wronged from whom you still need to seek forgiveness?

_____

_____

The debts we owe one another are like mere twenty-dollar bills compared to the infinite debt we owe our heavenly Father. Our posture should always be that of humility and brokenness, knowing we are undeserving. Brokenness is the road map by which we find our way back to an intimate relationship with God and compassion for one another.

To what degree is your life marked by brokenness?

_____

_____

_____

_____

Scripture tells us that pride is a grave sin. Think of some ways that pride hinders us of intimacy with God. Meditate on Psalm 51:17.

Prayer Journal:

When someone we love has hurt us, forgiveness can be exceptionally hard. Think of some offenses and hurts that have been particularly hard for you to release to God. Pray that you will become able to accept forgiveness as well as extend it.

Lord, I thank you for your mercy that is available to me every day. Help me to let go of . . .

_____

_____

_____

_____

_____

_____

_____

_____

_____

_____

_____

_____

LESSON EIGHT: The Armor

"And lead us not into temptation, but deliver us from the evil one."
(Matthew 6:13)

When you request that God "lead us not into temptation, but deliver us from the evil one," you should immediately remember to put on the full armor of God so that you can take your stand against the devil's schemes.

Read Ephesians 6:11–18. Identify and describe each piece of armor in this passage.

_____

_____

_____

_____

_____

_____

While it has become fashionable to credit the devil with every temptation we face, we must be ever mindful that spiritual warfare involves the world and the flesh as well. Sometimes we simply use the devil as our scapegoat. While the devil certainly "prowls around like a roaring lion looking for someone to devour" (1 Peter 5:8), it is imperative to remember that we are capable of choosing against God without the prodding of the devil.

Have you ever been guilty of subscribing to the devil-made-me-do-it theology? What do you think are the dangers of this kind of thinking?

_____

_____

_____

1 Corinthians 10:13 says that "No temptation has seized you except what is common to man. And God is faithful; he will not let you be tempted beyond what you can bear. But when you are tempted, he will also provide a way out so that you can stand up under it." How has God helped you to resist temptation in the past?

_____

_____

_____

The Bible says that Jesus was "tempted in every way, just as we are—yet was without sin" (Hebrews 4:15). Reflect on the amazing truth of the Incarnation—Jesus, though fully God, took on a human nature and overcame temptation, modeling for us a perfect, sinless life. In fact, it is Jesus' ability to sympathize with our human experience that the writer of Hebrews used as grounds for his encouragement that we can and should "approach the throne of grace with confidence, so that we may receive mercy and find grace to help us in our time of need" (Hebrews 4:16). Take some time now to thank God for the privilege of having direct access to him in prayer on account of the person and work of our great high priest, Jesus Christ.

Prayer Journal:

Read about how Jesus overcame the temptations of the devil in Matthew 4:1–11. As Jesus armed himself with the "sword of the Spirit, which is the word of God" (Ephesians 6:17), so must we. Think about how we should follow Christ's example of resisting temptation when we are tempted by the world, the flesh, or the devil.

Lord, give me strength to deny myself and follow you today. Help me resist . . .

_____

_____

_____

LESSON NINE: Into the Deep

"As the deer pants for streams of water, so my soul pants for you, O God." (Psalm 42:1)

Going deep with God begins with a major paradigm shift in our perceptions about prayer. Rather than looking for techniques through which we can get God to answer our prayers, we must be ever mindful that prayer is an opportunity for developing intimacy with the very One who knit us together in our mother's womb.

Are you guilty of wanting a relationship with God without the discipline of investing quality time?

_____

_____

_____

_____

_____

_____

Think about what your prayer life was before you started this study. What misconceptions did you have about prayer prior to this study?

_____

_____

_____

_____

_____

_____

"How precious to me are your thoughts, O God! How vast is the sum of them! Were I to count them, they would outnumber the grains of sand. When I awake, I am still with you." (Psalm 139:17–18)

How much of your prayer time do you spend just listening for God to speak to you? Do you feel that you are doing too much of the talking?

_____

_____

_____

_____

_____

_____

"You are my hiding place; you will protect me from trouble and surround me with songs of deliverance." (Psalm 32:7)

Think about someone in your life who exudes God's strength and wisdom. What do you know about that individual's prayer life? Identify the aspects of his or her prayer life that you would like to begin to model.

_____

_____

_____

_____

_____

God desires to answer his children when we pray. But often his answer is "wait." What prayers are you still waiting on? Why might God be wanting you to wait?

_____

_____

_____

_____

_____

Prayer Journal:

Relationships, whether with friends, family, or God, all require an investment of quality time in order to grow. Do you think that you are better disciplined in the area of prayer after this study? If you feel you are still struggling, ask the Lord for his continued help.

Lord, I treasure the privilege of being alone with you, and the quality time we have. I long to hear your voice. Please help me to . . .

_____

_____

_____

_____

_____

_____

_____

_____

_____

_____

_____

_____

_____

_____

_____

_____

_____

_____

_____

_____

_____

_____

_____

_____

_____

_____

LESSON TEN: Embracing the Prayer of Jesus

"Therefore everyone who hears these words of mine and puts them into practice is like a wise man . . ." (Matthew 7:24)

As stated before, "the secret to prayer is secret prayer." Your public presence is a direct reflection of your private prayer life. If you spend time in the secret place, you will exude peace in the midst of life's storms. Making space for prayer takes intentionality and discipline.

What has been the most challenging new concept or idea about prayer that you have encountered in these sessions?

_____

_____

_____

_____

_____

_____

List some goals you have for your prayer life. Make sure they are specific and something you are able to accomplish.

_____

_____

_____

_____

_____

_____

Do you believe that prayer is now a priority for you? Perhaps you feel that prayer was an essential part of your life before you began this study, and you were looking for ways to continue in your growth. God wants us to see prayer as a way to enjoy fellowship with him, no matter where we are in our prayer lives.

Think about your week. How does your schedule indicate that prayer is a priority to you? If you are neglecting the pleasure and practice of prayer, make it your goal to meet with the Lord in a quiet place every day for the next month.

_____

_____

_____

_____

_____

_____

What new insights about the Lord's Prayer have you gained that are particularly meaningful to you? Explain.

_____

_____

_____

_____

_____

_____

Now that you are at the end of this study, rate your prayer life on a scale of 1 to 10. Has it improved? Think of any remaining obstacles to your personal prayer life that can be removed to help you glorify God more and help you develop a more intimate relationship with him.

_____

_____

_____

_____

_____

_____

_____

Prayer Journal:

Prayer does allow us to touch heaven. Prayer is a beautiful fore-taste of something we will experience for all eternity—unbroken communion with God. There we will forever explore the glory and grandeur of his grace and greatness. We have so much to look forward to in our relationship with God. We can begin to experi-ence this communion with God even now by venturing out of the shallow waters of our askings and gettings and diving deep into the ocean of prayer. Now that we have seen that the Lord's Prayer is any-thing but a vain repetition or monotonous incantation, let us pray according to the pattern of the prayer of Jesus:

> Our Father in heaven,
> hallowed be your name,
> your kingdom come,
> your will be done
> on earth as it is in heaven.
> Give us today our daily bread.
> Forgive us our debts,
> as we also have forgiven our debtors.
> And lead us not into temptation,
> but deliver us from the evil one,
> for yours is the kingdom
> and the power and the glory forever.
> Amen.